# Dying to be Alive

# Dying to be Alive

C. Thomas Perry Ph.D.

Print information available on the last page.

Rev. date: 05/08/2020

**To order additional copies of this book, contact:**
Xlibris
1-800-455-039
www.Xlibris.com.au
Orders@Xlibris.com.au
722454

# Table of Contents

# Acknowledgements

I would like to thank my children for loving me throughout and supporting me unconditionally.

I would also like to recognize the assistance of Kevin Conner and his wife Rene, spiritual mentors and teachers over the years who offered sound advice and counsel with the content of this book. Since publishing the first edition both Kevin and Rene have gone to be with the Lord, I remember them with great affection.

At the time of writing the second edition I would also like to thank my fellow author and dearest friend, Kerryn Redpath, who has offered me much support and helped me to believe in the significance of this book in the face of considerable opposition.

# Introduction

It could happen to any of us, at any moment, in any place, in an instant. Death is a universal condition. It will happen to all of us one day. This book is an account of my encounter with death that became an encounter with eternity, with infinity and with new life. It also tells of the changes it brought about in my life, my understanding of God and my growing awareness that we all need to be freed from the shackles of our intellectually dominated world. It is an attempt to describe the indescribable and to put the unspeakable into words.

This project has been a journey of discovery as I have grappled with the challenge of converting an experience of the spirit into terms that I hope can, to some extent, translate the essential nature of the spiritual realm into the physical world. There is no doubt that writing this book has deepened my understanding of the death experience by forcing an evaluation of every aspect of my memory, the way in which my life has changed as a result of these events and the difficulties I have encountered in speaking out about issues of life beyond death. To write a book such as this takes more courage than you would imagine, as it brings with it accusations of delusion, or even worse, of fabrication of events for financial gain. The withdrawal (in January 2015) of another account of a death experience had the potential to do great damage on many fronts, but most particularly to detract from the credibility of all accounts of death experiences.

Firstly, I utterly disassociate myself from such deceptive practices and will stand by the authenticity of my story. I guess it is inevitable that sooner or later a false account will surface. The question to ask is whether the one false account should detract from the many other truthful stories. It makes me all the more determined to make my story known to the world and to tip the balance toward the authentic accounts that have given so many people hope in these dark times.

It is my intention that this book will go some of the way to restoring that breach of trust. Any reader has the right to be told the truth in a Christian publication and it is unfortunate that from this time forward, any account of a near-death encounter will be scrutinized intensely. I do not think this is entirely a bad thing as we should be sure as to the authentic nature of the book prior to publication. I am a man in my sixties, I hold a Ph.D. in Media and I am the father of five beautiful children. My life has not been perfect and there are many things I am ashamed of in my personal history, but this book is not one of them. I am proud to stand before the world and proclaim that there is life after death; that Jesus does exist and is eternally watching over us and is concerned for each of us on an individual basis.

I believe absolutely that there are spiritual powers of darkness that stand against this knowledge being distributed to the world. It has been my experience that circumstances have sometimes seemed to be very loaded against this book being written and at times it seemed as if the devil was on a personal mission to destroy my life before I could get this story out. Other authors have also been challenged in this way and I refer to Crystal McVea's book *Waking Up in Heaven*, 1 in which she refers to severe spiritual attacks on her life in an attempt to prevent her from sharing her story.

I for one am not happy to allow the darkness to overshadow the light. The events that occurred were very real, very powerful and very significant as a record of the things that are unseen, outside the physical world and under the oversight of Jesus himself. I believe the world needs to hear about God's love for us all, particularly in our time of dying. I do not claim this book to be proof of heaven, I do not think God ever intended us to be able to prove such things, but rather I am hoping to increase faith in God's infinite love, and his concern for each human being as they leave their mortal bodies and come into his presence. If my record can help any individual come to a closer relationship with God and increase their trust in him then I will be satisfied that it has achieved its goal. If it can help anyone to understand their daily walk with God in greater depth, then I will be happy that it has been effective.

I believe that it is God's will that as many people hear about this experience as possible and I will make every effort to spread the word as effectively as I am able. I trust that God will help me on this journey and that the Holy Spirit will accompany every reading of this book to open the understanding of the reader to experience some measure of the wonder, the power and infinite glory of God. I have been in the presence of Jesus and I can assure the reader that this experience is indeed a pearl of great price and that nothing in this world compares to the love that can be felt when you stand in the presence of the Master. I entrust this book to you in the hope that it will connect with you, open your eyes to new possibilities and lift you into the presence of Jesus himself, even as I was lifted. May God bless you as you read and may the doubts and intellectual restraints fall away as your spirit encounters the hope of a life to come.

# PART ONE
## EXPERIENCE

# Chapter 1

## Through the Veil

The pains in my chest had been gradually building for over a week. Not the sharp stabbing pain you would imagine would accompany a heart complaint; more of a slowly building tight, cramping sensation that was made worse by activity. I knew enough to act on this warning sign, so visited the local doctor to have my heart checked out. She seemed fairly concerned but by no means panicked by my symptoms and suggested a few tests to see what may be happening in that ailing chest of mine. It could have been musculo-skeletal pain, but the fact that the pain increased with exertion was not a good sign.

On Monday, I lost a patch of chest hair, shaved for the ECG sensor, watched as my nurse recorded a few seconds of my pulse and sent off the results for analysis. The results were expected back in a week. The doctor suggested I take it very easy in the meantime and avoid any major exertion, just as a precaution. On Friday, I rang to see if the results were in. They had not been processed and I was still left in the dark as to the cause of my pain. I was content that this was all precautionary and proceeded to get on with my life at a slightly reduced pace. The symptoms had decreased somewhat, I felt that perhaps there was improvement and that maybe I was suffering from some kind of unusual lung infection. In short, I was well on the way to convincing myself that there was nothing at all wrong with me and that all would be fine within a few days. In hindsight, I think that obeying doctor's orders of relaxing and taking it easy to look after myself, had given me a false sense of security and the illusion of considerable improvement.

On Sunday I felt almost up to doing some work in the garden so headed out to start some tidying up with the line trimmer. At the best of times starting this stubborn machine can be difficult. This day it reached new heights of resistance, refusing to sputter into life no matter how I tugged the starting cord. After about five minutes of this, I noticed the sensation in my chest had increased and with a few more pulls on the cord I was in no doubt. The cramping sensation was now a painful and palpable throbbing in the centre of my chest, and with my limited knowledge of all matters medical, I reasoned that this was not a very good scenario; alone in the back garden of my house, cramps in the chest, feeling decidedly unusual and nobody to call to for help.

Hearing a voice talking to me clearly from within my head, is not altogether unknown for me amongst the turbulent traffic grid of swirling thoughts, but today, this voice was clear, powerful and urgent.

*"You are going to die but I have some things for you to do."*

It certainly got my attention, but there did seem to be a major problem in the underlying logic of this statement. To die is one thing, to have things to do seems somehow to be slightly contradictory. I had a pretty good idea who was talking to me.

"OK Lord, what should I do?" I replied.

*"Go inside and call the ambulance straight away."*

Immediately I was on the phone and the emergency operator dispatched an ambulance with a minimum of fuss. I calmly packed a few clothes in a travel bag and waited. The pain did not diminish. I was afraid and yet strangely calm in the moment with the sort of stillness I had experienced before in moments of crisis. Shock has this effect on me; I had a fair idea that God was there right beside me, leading me through the critical time of waiting.

The ambulance crew were at the door in a few minutes, one hardened warrior and another on his first mission of mercy. The young one spoke to me about the symptoms and was in some doubt as to whether it was actually a heart attack but decided to treat it as such as a precautionary measure. The treatment involved an injection of morphine and administering nitro glycerol to lower my blood pressure. I remembered a warning my mother had given me that she had reacted negatively to morphine on one occasion and informed the ambulance officer, but he did not seem too concerned.

Within a few minutes they had me prepared, on the trolley and were wheeling me to the ambulance. I had installed a ramp at the front of my house to help gain access for my daughter, who was permanently wheelchair bound after being involved in a tragic car accident when she was seven years of age. This was probably the only moment I had ever felt good about having that ramp at the front of my house.

Once in the back of the ambulance, the journey began. The senior officer drove the ambulance while the junior stayed with me in the back, checking blood pressure and pulse rate and talking me through the procedure. He injected me with another dose of morphine and administered more nitro tablets, warning me that I may become a bit dizzy after this second dosage. Sure enough, I became disoriented and dizzy and told him I felt as if I would pass out. The world span and I blacked out.

\*　\*　\*

It was a sleepy, calm sensation and I felt myself drifting slowly downward, as if falling into a nap on a summer afternoon. I started to give in to the weightless gliding and was ready to simply fall asleep. The gradual descent was strangely alluring and yet something was nagging at the back of my mind that all was not well. There was no awareness of what had just occurred, but this slow drift felt like all I had ever known, or would know.

I then became aware of the vast vacuum of darkness beneath me and fear began to grip my soul. One awareness became clearly present in my mind; that this slow descent may not end well. At this point, I cried out with all my being for help; a resounding scream for attention, "Jesus help me".

I continued to drift and was increasingly aware of the sense of infinite darkness and void beneath me. I had a strong feeling that if I continued to drift, the fall may never end or may end in a dark, desolate lifeless place.

This was more of an emotional realization than any logical reasoning, more of a feeling than a knowing: I was for the first time aware of the experience of being a soul outside a body, of pure thought without a brain shaping, limiting or directing the content of my thoughts.

At that moment, my arm was caught in a strong, vice like grip and I was pulled quite sharply in an upward direction. I should explain at this time, that there was an awareness of up and down but no sensation of weight or gravity. Have you ever floated underwater and allowed yourself to slowly drift in the pleasant weightless caress of the aquatic world? That sensation is the most similar to what I experienced at this moment. I knew up and I knew down, but I was totally at the mercy of the hand that grasped me and steadily lifted me higher. I had no power to alter my course or direction, or to influence the events that were taking place.

A voice spoke and yet it did not speak. I knew what was said yet I did not hear it with my ears. I was aware of it deep within myself; another mind was entering mine and filling me with its thoughts. *"You don't want to go that way"* it said, referring to the dark abyss below. The ascent continued for a while. I had little comprehension of time and in fact the whole environment felt strangely free of, and separate from time. My vision was not clear, everything around me seemed foggy and blurred, swirling in an undefined mist of fragments and wisps of white and grey. I could sense a growing light and became aware that there were several indistinct shapes gathering around me that I knew to be angels. They were cloaked in a dim glow and I felt extremely small in their presence. I was also sharply aware of being observed by others who were not visible at the time, but I knew these souls. This was my family, those who had passed on in years gone by and I could feel their presence; I could sense grandparents, aunties, uncles, cousins and others I had not met but who I presumed were my ancestors. The awareness of their presence brought back childhood memories of extended family gatherings. It was a feeling of complete familiarity, oneness and companionship, of being in the presence of those I belonged with.

How can I describe the sensation I was experiencing at that time? Do you have any memory of your earliest childhood moments of being held and caressed by your mother, or a person you loved and adored more than any other? The warmth of love, the glowing satisfaction and the knowledge that you loved that person completely and this was a perfect moment that you never wanted to stop? My chest felt as if it would explode with the power and completeness of the love that welled up within me. I was floating on my back in mid-air, space, water, or whatever it was, totally overpowered by this blissful sensation. It remains to this day as the most perfect moment of my entire existence; such peace, such love, such contentment! Drifting in love, feeling the presence of these immensely powerful, intelligent and beautiful angelic beings that huddled nearby discussing my presence among them. Although I could not distinguish all their thoughts, I could somehow understand fragments of the communications passing between them. This went on for some time, if you could call it time. I have no idea how long this lasted before I started to become aware of my surroundings and my vision became slightly clearer.

"Where am I? What's happening to me?"

With this statement, one of the beings approached me and began to communicate, one to one. I would not describe it as speech; it was a far more profound experience than a normal conversation. It was as if I knew the whole mind of the speaker as he directed his thoughts into me. And what a mind! I felt the knowledge and wisdom of the ages in his presence and was awestruck by his power, gentleness and love. It was as if every kind, loving or admirable quality was amplified enormously in this being. More than that, I felt through the connection between our minds that I had access to all that had ever been, or ever would be. All events, past, present and future seemed to be accessible through this incredible being. There did not seem to be the same distinctly linear timeline on which we travel in our daily lives. Time had become somehow like a tangible object which could be observed as one would look down on a landscape from above and simultaneously see below, behind and ahead. I felt the weight of generations, the call of future destinies and the current unfolding of events contained in his consciousness that continued to emanate the most profound sensations into my soul.

I consider myself to be reasonably intelligent, having a PhD in my field and having worked as a university lecturer for some years, but in his presence, I felt less than an infant in mental and emotional capacity. He read me like a book, he looked straight through me and saw every aspect of my being and I was completely naked, raw and exposed to his gaze, aware that he was simply observing me in a way I had never thought possible. This brought to mind a statement from the Apostle Paul, who said, "Now we see but a poor reflection as in a mirror; then we shall see face to face. Now I know in part; then I shall know fully, even as I am known." [I Cor.13;12 NIV]

All this occurred in what seemed like a fraction of a second, an instant realization of the nature of infinity, an encounter with the "all loving" and the "all knowing" as my soul was joined with his in a glorious union. Nothing compares to this! I have never felt truly complete for one instant since this happened, and I do not think I have ever been able to truly enjoy my life to the full since then. Every happy moment, every earthly pleasure, every warm companion I have experienced since that moment has not been nearly enough to fill my desperate need to revisit this time in his presence. Just to be with him has changed me forever. Words can in no way begin to describe the power, the magnificence and the overwhelming love that coursed through my being.

As accurately as I can paraphrase thoughts into words, he said *"You have died, and we are now deciding what to do with you. If you are given the choice, would you like to remain here forever or return to your earthly existence? We could provide you a place here until the end or you could return."*

Surprisingly, this created quite a dilemma for me. As a father of children, one of them being only eight years old at the time, I obviously had them in the forefront of my mind. I also had a twenty eight year old daughter with profound brain injury who would be heartbroken if I did not return. It seems obvious from the earthly perspective, of course, that I would return. The reality of being there in his presence however, was so overwhelmingly beautiful that I had to wrestle with my growing desire to stay there always. I could imagine no more perfect state to be in for eternity than the way I felt at that moment.

I considered my children, I considered that I felt a strong sense of an unfinished business in my life, that I had a strong belief that God has a mission for me to fulfil on Earth, especially considering the voice that spoke with me at the onset of the heart attack and other words of prophecy that had been spoken over my life.

Then the reality of death and dying impacted on my mind and all the earthly fears associated with dying began to rise within me. I began to panic, shouting that I could not leave my life, that I had to be there for my children, that I had not completed my job on earth. My distress drew immediate attention from the other glowing angelic beings, who quickly approached and inquired as to my condition. They seemed more than a little disturbed by my behaviour. They explained that these emotions of fear, panic or distress were not usual in this place and that they radiated the wrong power into the atmosphere.

The beautiful one I had been communicating with, asked me to be calm, explained again that they were not accustomed to fear in that place and that it caused a disruption. I began to calm myself with some intervention from the angels who seemed imperceptibly to assist me in that process. Once calm, I said to him,

"I choose to return, as I feel the need to complete my task as a father and to complete my deeds on Earth."

He replied, *"There is some risk involved in this, as you would, if you remained, be granted eternal paradise, but if you return, I cannot guarantee that would be the case when you eventually die. You will encounter many difficulties and temptations when you return to that life."*

I responded by reaffirming my decision, expressing my need to be there for my children. He then approached the angelic beings and said to one of them, *"See if the vessel is good for him to return."*

The angel then flew from our presence, not with wings, but he simply drifted away and curiously, I could see as if in the distance my body in the ambulance trolley with the angel moving around and examining the body closely. He returned after a short while and said; *"The vessel is good."* The first powerful being who had lifted me up earlier then said, *"Prepare yourself and we will send you back to your earthly body".*

At this point curiosity arose in me and I began to ask questions. "Who are you?"

*"I am the one you call Lord"*

"Lord, is this heaven?"

*"We are outside the realm of heaven here. This is the space souls pass through on their journey. I have come here to meet you and to see that you are sent on safely."*

"What of my future Lord? What do I have to do?"

*"That is to be acted out in your life on earth. Your life is not written, it depends on the choices you make and how well you act on your opportunities. I would have you do several things in the world, but it is up to you to do them."*

"What things would you have me do?"

*"There are many, you have much to do for God's kingdom, but you should tell them about this."*

"What, about being here?"

*"Yes, there are many who need to hear about this place, about the path to heaven and the void below. They need to know of the free gift they are offered."*

At this point I was simply overcome with his magnificence and I fell before him, reaching out to touch him. Once again, he took my hand, this time lifting me up on my feet. This was the first time

I had been upright while in that place, as I had been floating on my back or side the entire time. I was surprised to realize that he was about the same size as me, despite a sense of his immensity and I realized that this enormous presence emanated from his spiritual power and authority, not from any physical stature.

*"There is little time, we must send you back now before damage occurs."*

He then led me a short distance to where the angels were gathered, apparently watching events unfolding and discussing among themselves things that I did not understand. These angelic beings approached the Lord and were discussing with him something to do with my future. One of them said to the Lord,

*"He should be told."*

At that, the Lord approached me and said,

*"There are things you need to know about events that will take place when you return to your body. You are going to meet a woman. This is not written, but the meeting has the potential to be dangerous to your journey and she could draw you away from me or could be drawn toward me by you. This is one of the tasks you must undertake."*

"Lord couldn't this be avoided if it is dangerous for me?"

He replied, *"Some events are already in motion and will not be reshaped. It will occur. What is in question is what you will make of the time when you return."*

I then understood that the danger he spoke of was to do with my purity as a soul, that my existence on earth was by its very nature, impure and that any soul entering heaven, was judged by a standard that no earthly being could meet unless covered by the mercy of God. To re-enter the battleground of life on earth was to be exposed to a greater risk than any of us here can really comprehend unless we have felt the perspective that comes from a spiritual, angelic view of our existence.

The Lord continued,

*"Be strong and remember I am always with you. Call for help from me when you need it and I will be there."*

I then found myself floating again, this time the sensation of being underwater was far clearer. I could see a light above me and I 'swam' toward the light, desperately lunging to reach the surface and take a breath of air. Suddenly I broke the surface of the water, emerged into the bright light, took a huge gasp of air, and looked around me.

The junior ambulance officer was standing over me, wide eyed and looking considerably panicked.

"I see you are back with us," he said.

I lay there completely overwhelmed by the heaviness of my body, the pain in my chest and all the physical sensations that had been absent for the last few minutes. Everything felt confused, clumsy, oppressive and dark after the beautiful lightness of being no more than a soul with no physical body. Every part of my body felt as if it weighed heavily on me and the overall feeling of impurity was palpable. I felt corrupted simply by being here. I felt the force of physical existence as a powerful restraint on the freedom of my spirit that I had felt beforehand. The pain in my chest was very strong and yet one thing had changed. All my fear had gone. Prior to the near death experience I had been in considerable fear of the outcome and now I felt a quiet inner confidence and peace that if I were to die the destination would be far more pleasant than the current physical prison.

"They sent me back........ I saw angels."

The ambulance officer looked a little startled and he started to explain to the senior ambulance officer that I had been "asystolic," a term I later discovered meant that I had no heartbeat. He told me that he had applied CPR, which had failed to revive me, had removed my shirt and was about to use the defibrillator. He apologized as he had applied CPR very firmly and had "heard some cracking", possible some cracked ribs. I have suffered from a fair amount of pain in my sternum since that time. He also said that he had thrown the shirt in the corner as it was sopping wet. He passed me the shirt and I said,

"But this shirt is completely dry!"

He looked quite shocked and felt the dry shirt for himself.

We continued our journey to the hospital and I was admitted to emergency, wired up with ECG sensors and monitored closely for the next 8 hours. During this time I was sharply aware of the things I had experienced while out of my body. I felt the presence of angels watching me consistently for the next few days. Occasionally I could hear their voices whispering to me. One said to me; "We have healed three arteries, but one we cannot. That will have to be repaired."

I did not understand what was happening at the time, but now I understand that my perceptions of the spiritual world were heightened through having been in that realm. It was as if I was separated from the world of the angels by the thinnest of fabrics, with angels peeping through the veil to monitor my wellbeing and progress through the hospital treatment. The presence of God was strong and I could feel his power surrounding me constantly.

After many hours of waiting in a small bay in the emergency ward I was finally transferred to the cardiac ward. Further tests were performed and eventually the enzyme that indicated that a heart attack had taken place was detected in my blood and I was given an angiogram to observe the source of the blockage. This involved inserting a camera device through the artery in my groin and feeding the tube up into my heart. I was fully conscious during the entire process and sure enough, a blockage was detected in an artery and they decided to insert a stent to rectify the problem. The surgeon did comment that she thought it appeared that I had undergone angioplasty in the past, which involves expanding the arteries at the blockage point in a ballooning type of action. I assured them this was not the case, but the voice that had told me of the healed arteries was very present in my mind. Another doctor commented to me, "It appears you are one of the lucky ones who are able to grow new arteries around the old blockages." Once again I could not help wondering if these were the three healings the angels had mentioned to me.

A stent was inserted; a process which I was able to feel within my heart and the relief from pain was immediate once the blockage was repaired. The sensation of a mechanical probe inserted through one's arteries into the interior of the heart is certainly a disconcerting experience and yet the immense relief as the blockage was removed and blood flow restored was both instant and profound. The nagging pain that had been a constant factor in my life for over a week was finally relieved and I could once again relax in the knowledge that my heart was pumping effectively.

It is difficult to explain the effect a heart attack has on a person's confidence and sense of self. It is as close to the central essence of one's self as a physical organ can be. I had not realized how much my heart was connected with my identity. How we humans take for granted that our hearts will keep on beating, that life will simply go on as it always has and that our strength and health are a given. The realization that there was not only a hope of full recovery, but every chance that I would function more effectively than I had for some time with full blood flow through the arteries of my heart lifted my spirits and I started to look forward to a second chance at life.

My three younger children and former wife came to visit me that day and I had seen on the faces of my children such concern and love for me that I was glad to have made the choice to return to this body and continue my life. My understanding of the importance of love had been changed forever. Love was the very essence of heaven; it flowed through my being still, as if a residue of the spiritual realm had remained within my being and continued to surge within my body like a dynamo of electrical energy.

Despite my physical condition, the spiritual elation I had experienced had also remained with me and, it coursed through my being on many levels, heart, mind body and soul. I clearly felt the presence of God observing, loving and nurturing me and could recognize the angelic presences in my vicinity and although no visible sign of their presence was seen, I know they were watching me closely at that time.

This became even more apparent once I had my Bible with me in hospital. I have always believed in God's power working through the words of that book, guiding us toward particular verses which are meant for an individual in a particular circumstance, to give instruction, comfort and solace. I opened the book with all the memories of the heavenly experience clearly in my mind and it was as if every page I turned to was specifically targeted at my life, at that particular moment. The first verse that I flicked the pages open to was Psalm 30:

"I will exalt you O Lord, for you lifted me out of the depths and did not let my enemies gloat over me. O Lord my God I called for you to help and you healed me. O Lord you bought me up from the grave; you spared me from going down to the pit." [Ps. 30:1-3 NIV]

This was followed by a coincidental encounter with the record of Jesus raising Lazarus from the dead, Paul proclaiming victory over death and other verses immediately relating to the power of God to overcome death. It was as if the personal experience I had undergone was somehow linked spiritually to the turning of the pages and I could not open the Bible to a verse that did not relate to being set free from the grave or released from death. It was as if God's hand was on my every action, arranging time and space to open the pages I needed right at that moment to confirm his hand in my every circumstance. I will never forget the comfort and warmth that brought to me.

Although my initial experience was over, the pathway it opened up was only just beginning and little did I know I was about to set off on the road that has led my feet to the current days through times of joy, of despair, of occasionally feeling that the Lord had abandoned me and other times knowing that his hand was on me over the entire journey. I now know with all my being that there was never a time when his all-knowing awareness did not see every mistake, victory, failing, success and also every insignificant moment in my life. Being able to "know as I am known" has forever changed my understanding of God's involvement in our daily lives on an intimate and personal level and of the participation of the angels in our passage through time and space.

The invisible hand of God is a most powerful force, which always intervenes when required, and watches tirelessly over those he loves to pick them up when they fall, or to nudge them this way or that to avoid pitfalls and place them in the path he wishes them to travel.

As two days in hospital went by and I was starting to feel far better, my mind continually turned back to the experience I had undergone. I was desperately lonely, having been divorced for almost three years and living on my own. I cried out to God, praying for someone to love, as I did not want to go on living that lonely existence. Almost immediately I was given a vivid vision of a woman's face. The Lord spoke quietly to me again. "This is the woman I will give you. She is within a kilometer of you right now." I was quite happy to accept that promise and first met this woman three weeks later. I had been looking to find a relationship via the internet but I had given up all hope of having any success, particularly after the heart attack and was planning on removing myself from the internet site that day, when I received an email from her.

I explained my rather damaged condition to her, just out of hospital, five children, one of them severely brain injured and me needing time to recover. We agreed to meet and go out for a meal together. When I went to pick her up in my car, sure enough, she lived about 800 meters from the hospital where I lay.

# Chapter 2

## Rethinking

The return to the earthly plane brought about many adjustments, questions and evaluations concerning my experience in the spiritual body. I was immediately wondering what effect this would have on my physical existence and the way I would live my life from that time forward. I had heard of other people experiencing near death experiences, their encounters with the throne room, God seated on the throne, with legions of angels surrounding him. My experience did seem somewhat smaller in scale and yet no less significant in its impact on my understanding of God and his relationship with me as an individual.

I had somehow expected Jesus to appear with some identifiable regalia, a crown, a scepter, a blinding light or some other powerful manifestation of his glory. My meeting with him however, was not characterized by external indicators of his divinity. The power of his presence was evident in the profound effect he had on my heart, my spirit and my emotions. He seemed to occupy a position of intermediation between humanity and angels, having a deeper understanding of the human condition than they did and yet his level of authority was obviously high above theirs. This was evident in the respect and awe directed toward him by the angels around me while I was in his presence. This was a being that not only ruled in the spiritual realm, but also one who could reach into the depths of human experience and know it intimately. It was this quality that was the most noticeable difference between him and the angels.

I spent almost the entire duration of my death experience in his presence, from the moment I was carried upward by his hand, until my return to the body. It is therefore difficult to discern whether the feelings of overpowering love and wellbeing were just a part of the fabric of that place, or whether they were emanating from his presence. The experience of joining with him in communication, the speech of the spirit I described in the previous chapter, certainly bought with it a flood of emotion, as well as an enormous depth of awareness and knowledge. The power of love seemed to flow out from him as an inevitable result of being in his presence. To be in his vicinity was to be washed over with waves of warm love that erupted from within my chest and flowed through my entire being. The sensation I experienced brought to mind the episode in the Garden of Gethsemane, when the soldiers came to arrest Jesus and were suddenly confronted with the measure of his majesty, which resulted in them falling to the ground in the face of such overwhelming power. Indeed, at one stage I did find myself prostrated before him simply overcome by the dimensions of his love and power.

Having spent some considerable amount of time in my life as a student of the Bible, I had come to a certain theoretical, academic understanding of the position of authority occupied by the risen Christ. Meeting him in person has profoundly altered my conception of his current role in the heavens. I had thought of him enthroned in glory at the right hand of the Father ruling with him in the throne room, with angels doing his bidding. I imagined his omniscience, as he understood all that occurred in the universe from one location in time and space and I had mentally built a picture of how that would appear.

My short time with him has brought me to understand his role in a different way, as a statement or a title of his position of authority. Just as a President or Prime Minister of a nation has an official role that is represented by their official presence and position in the White House or the Houses of Parliament and yet they have a personal, more private existence on many other levels; individual appointments, a family life, office staff, *etc.*, it is similar with Jesus Christ. He does indeed occupy a position of glory, very evident in his revered position of leadership there, yet he also functions outside that throne room in his unlimited role as the Son of God. It is his right to occupy the throne, yet it is also his right to travel through the universe as he pleases. He was there mingling with the angels and with me, a poor mortal human in transit.

He has appeared to countless people on earth and is intimately acquainted with earthly events. The words of Jesus to his disciples are very informative. He said, "You will see the angels ascending and descending upon the Son of Man." [John 1:51] Note that he does not say that the angels are ascending to and from the Christ, but that they are ascending and descending *upon* him. He is actively engaged in the daily communication between heaven and earth. The angels utilize his power and presence to fulfil their function as messengers to and from God and humanity. This was the sort of incredible power I observed in his ability to command the angels to come and go to observe and report on events on earth.

As I readjusted to life in the physical body with the added awareness I had received in the spiritual world I came to several realizations. Foremost among them was the understanding that the voice of Jesus had been far more audible in my life over a far longer period than I had believed to be the case. The speech of the spirit, or telepathic communication, I had experienced with him had not entirely ceased with my return to the body. I could at times still feel and discern the presence and the voice of Jesus whispering gently in my busy mind. Having felt his presence and been in his immediate vicinity I could now identify a particular identity and personality in the communication. In the same way as I have at times in my life known that someone I love was approaching, or nearby, although I could not see or hear them, I could now sense his presence far more clearly than before.

Many teachers have spoken on the theme of the "still, small voice" [I Kings 19:12 KJV] or "gentle whisper" of God's voice [I

Kings 19:12 NIV]. This can be most effectively heard only when we still the chatter of our minds and allow God to speak into a quiet space. What I now realized was that his voice had been present both prior to and now, even more clearly heard after the death experience. What had changed was that I now had a reference point from which I could evaluate and identify the characteristics of his voice given that I had met with the person to whom this voice belongs. I know the speaker, which makes identifying the voice far easier.

I now understand that the voice of God is easily accessible and he is a readily available conversation partner. He awaits our effort and participation in the conversation, developing in ourselves the ability to give precedence to his voice over the normal everyday thoughts that cloud and fill our minds. We are constantly full of self-centered chatter, incessant mental debate, the discussions and arguments that bounce around within our minds. What I now realized was that I was in a unique position to identify his voice, not that I was any more advanced in controlling my mind and spirit, but that I now had the ability to identify the voice far more easily and clearly hear his words. I now knew the personality of Jesus within the voice that spoke gently within my mind. This is not an external, audible voice, but a gentle train of thought that comes from outside of your own being but can be heard within. This is an inner room that can be visited any time you choose to close off the dripping tap of your own mental chatter.

Jesus clearly gave many indications of his closeness and the ready availability of his presence and voice to those who are willing to make the effort to truly listen.

"Whoever has ears, let them hear." [Matt. 11:15 NIV]
"That I myself may be in them" [John :26 NIV]
"The Kingdom of God is within you" [Luke 17:21 KJV]

The most common form of prayer in today's Christianity involves a one- way flow of communication from the human who prays to the divine God. There is little expectation of direct response, let alone the possibility of a conversational exchange between humanity and God. If we are to take the quotes above seriously, there should indeed be the very real possibility of conversation with God. If we make the effort to listen with receptive ears to the whispering voice of wisdom that quietly offers us advice, help, comfort and support in our daily lives and we truly believe that God is serious about the words he sent to his prophets and the words spoken by Jesus on earth, then this conversation can become a central part of our day to day faith.

"Whether you turn to the right or to the left your ears will hear a voice behind you, saying 'This is the way; walk in it.'" [Isaiah 30:21 NIV]

"Then the eyes of those who see will no longer be closed and the ears of those who hear will listen." [Isaiah 32:3 NIV]

Why should the eyes of those who see need to be opened? Why should the ears of those who hear need to listen? The prophet is speaking of an inner spiritual awareness of God's words and vision that are integral to a person entering into God's kingdom while here on earth. Jesus used this concept repeatedly during his teaching. He spoke of the ears of spiritual listening, the eyes of spiritual vision. God is instructing us to open our inner eyes, listen with our inner ears.

The experience of communication with Jesus in person has led me to a deeper understanding of many statements that he made on earth, as are recorded in the Gospels. The Gospel of John includes Jesus' final prayers with his disciples, in which he says, "That all of them may be one, Father, just as you are in me and I am in you." [John 17:21 NIV] This suggests a situation where the level of unity that is enjoyed by Jesus and his Father is also possible for those who believe in him. Have you ever really stopped to consider the scale and significance of that statement? What an immense, all-encompassing unity is available to us if we only learn to hear the words of God with our inner ears and see with the eyes of the spirit.

The complete unity of mind and spirit I experienced with Jesus when he communicated with me in the spiritual realm is a potential state of being for us, here and now, in our earthly lives.

I find that thought incredibly exciting. Jesus worked with his disciples to train them in experiencing unity, to enable them to become one. Jesus was not suggesting a mere unity of ideas and concepts, not even a sense of friendship that helped the disciples to feel close to each other, although that certainly existed. The level of oneness he enjoyed with the Father was a complete union of the spirit. When Jesus declared, "Anyone who has seen me has seen the Father," [John 14:9 NIV] he was describing a unity so complete he expressed it as a union of identities.

There have been moments in my life, particularly after the death experience, when I have actually felt the thoughts of other people. Jesus himself was clearly able to sense the thoughts of others. An example of this was when Jesus forgave the sins of a man he was about to heal:

Jesus knew what they were thinking and asked, "Why are you thinking these things in your hearts"? [Luke 5:22 NIV]

I have observed this gift at work among group prayer sessions, when two or more people reach such a level of spiritual unity that they have supernaturally known things about each other, sensed secret or hidden fears and doubts, or have unearthed personal histories in a way that can only be explained by the unifying power of the Holy Spirit at work among the group. This is an example of the sort of unity Jesus was describing in his final prayer; "That all of them may be one, Father, just as you are in me and I am in you." [John 17:21 NIV]

I have had the incredible privilege to have experienced this unifying power first-hand with the Lord and that experience has left me with a clear awareness of this spiritual unity when it does occur. The nature of Christ is not unavailable to us; in fact, it was his explicit promise that we would share in his nature. In order to reach that level of unity we must learn to surrender our mental processes to his control and be willing to let go of our self-reliance enough to enter into direct communication with him. This possibility is in no way limited to near death experiences, but is available to those who firstly, are able to believe in the possibility and secondly, are able to believe that it is occurring in the here and now not in a historical document, but in real time, in your life, even as you read these words.

The apostle Paul certainly knew of this relationship. "We have the mind of Christ." [I Corinthians 2:16 NLT] This is not a figurative or metaphorical statement, but a literal testimony from Paul, who had experienced directly the actual spiritual presence of Jesus. Paul believed in a direct spiritual connection with the Lord through the Holy Spirit that revealed the mind of Christ to us in matters of judgement, wisdom and understanding.

The mind of Jesus can be literally within us if we remove the barriers of doubt and intellectual control. Those of you reading these words may even as you read be able to sense a rising surge of excitement and recognition, becoming aware of a benevolent force, sensing him within your heart and may hear a calm, encouraging voice prompting you to travel further along this way. This is the mind of Christ at work within you.

Coming to understand the nature of Jesus is quite literally equivalent to getting to know a person in your life, with the obvious difference that he already knows you intimately. The intention of this chapter is to clearly indicate the importance of recognizing his presence within you. The true impact of the death experience in my life has not been the immediate response to the experience itself, but rather the ongoing transformation that has occurred and continues to occur in my spiritual life. Several years have passed since the event and yet I have been gradually transformed and restored over that time. That is not to say there have not been times of despair and grief. Despite these times, which are an inevitable part of the human condition, there has been consistent growth in my spiritual awareness brought on by the sure knowledge that the spiritual realm, the heavens, the angels and the Lord are a very real if invisible presence in my daily life and within my soul.

The initial realization that the earthly physical existence is of *secondary* importance in the universal plan of God, has opened up a rich vein of research, exploration and highly targeted prayer with the goal of accessing the heavenly kingdom from within this life, this body, this physical world. Jesus' statement that "the

Kingdom of God is within you," [Luke 17:21 NIV] and Paul's claim that "Don't you know that you yourselves are God's temple and that God's Spirit dwells in your midst?" [I Cor. 3:16 NIV] has become the central theme of an ongoing, all-consuming search in my spiritual life.

Since that initial realization as to the scale of the insignificance of the physical existence when contrasted with the spiritual, several questions have continued to play on my mind.

- Where does God's temple and Spirit exist within me?
- How can I fully access it here and now?
- Are there prayers or meditations I can use that will bring the kingdom of heaven into my life in greater measure?

One thing that has become abundantly clear to me on this search is that the original voice of God that said to me "You are going to die, but I have some things for you to do," has become in a sense a self-fulfilling prophecy, as I would expect from God's voice in my life. The death experience has become a driving force within me to discover more, to remain receptive to the voice of God and to share my experience and the way in which God has led me since that time with as many as have "ears to hear."

I have been reticent to come forward and write this book, or to speak out about this experience for several reasons. Firstly, I do not feel worthy to put myself up as an example or teacher on this matter; secondly, people tend to look at you as if you were crazy when you share with them about such things. Despite this, gradually, over time the flame of God's Spirit within me has burned brighter and the imperative for spreading the message God has placed within me has increased so that I can no longer deny the urgency of publishing this information in any way I can.

Having the reference point of having been there has given me the decided advantage of being able to *feel* the kingdom of heaven and recognize its presence in a very literal sense. Just as one can sense the smell of a perfume, feel a change in the temperature of a change of mood in a person, I have found that I am now able to discern the presence of God's Kingdom as a very real, literal and identifiable spiritual presence.

Some of the identifiable factors I have observed which are conducive to the coming of the Kingdom on earth are:

- A genuine heart or intention, a willingness to listen for God's voice
- A motivation of love and the wellbeing of others
- A thirst to find out more about God
- An awareness of God's spiritual power as a *reality at work in the world*
- Belief in God and Jesus as *present* within a room, place or person
- Acceptance of strong emotions and other sensations as a sign of experiencing God's presence

The combination of the elements listed above consistently create an environment that "smells" like the kingdom of heaven … and it smells good.

"For where two or three gather together as my followers, I am there among them." [Matthew 18:20 NLT]

For many Christians and indeed for many other people, the sense of God's presence takes the form of a suspicion that "Yes I think God may be here." Without wanting to make myself out to be anything above any other person, I can honestly and humbly say that since my time with him I can to some extent now recognize and know the heavenly presence through the recollection of that experience. I am now able to declare "Yes I know that presence, I know that personality, I know that Spirit." This has become one of the most important indicators I have responded to when seeking out the presence of the kingdom of heaven on earth. Does this *feel* like his presence? Is this how I remember the Lord feeling to me?

The most important part of engaging with this process is not to go through rituals, or to observe religious rules. What really matters at the core of the experience is to know God. Not as a concept, not as an ideal, but to know him as a reality within you and as a central part of your life. He brings certain qualities with him, and the foremost of these is love. Please do not mistake this book for a call to adhere to religious precepts. It is a call to move beyond precepts or intellect and enter a relationship with the eternal God. It is an invitation to move beyond your comfort zone and dare to believe in the invisible power of God, Jesus and the angels. More than that it is intended to encourage you to invoke the kingdom of heaven and choose to be a part of its presence on this planet.

"May your Kingdom come soon. May your will be done on earth, as it is in Heaven." [Matthew 6:10 NLT]

These words have taken on a whole new meaning for me. Within the pages of this book are my humble attempts to explain, to discover, to explore and to invoke the kingdom of heaven here within my life and within the physical universe in which we all find ourselves existing. Dear reader, I invite you to journey on the way everlasting and invite the presence of God and his kingdom into your life, your body, soul heart and mind. His presence is with you right now!

# Chapter 3

## Time is no More

As we move towards the final goal of opening our awareness to the voice and presence of God, it is important that we come to understand the immensity and power of the force we are dealing with. This helps in developing a strong belief in his ability to do all things, to be within you, to speak to all of humanity and know every hair on our head. God is all, and in all, and to come to a full comprehension of his awesome scale and dimension opens the possibility of believing in those things we have been taught to believe are impossible. In the Western world we have been trained in doubt, taught to question, encouraged to reject anything outside the physical realm of existence and immersed in teachings that ridicule the spiritual. In order to counter this inbuilt skepticism I would now like to discuss further the realization and awareness that flooded into my being while I was in the presence of the Lord and in the spiritual body.

One of the most intriguing aspects of the death experience was the way in which time was perceived in the spiritual realm. In our earthly existence we think of time as an all-encompassing consistent and inflexible dimension. We assume that time passes at a constant rate as we move forward into an unknown future and away from a completed past. We have been taught to assume there is no way of knowing what is to come or altering the effects of what has been.

My experience of being momentarily united with the Lord of all has profoundly changed my understanding of time. Firstly, the idea that time is a consistent progression from past to future at a fixed rate, with an isolated moment we call "the present" in which we exist, must be examined more closely.

In the heavenly realm time is most definitely not experienced in the same manner. I was able to glimpse a few moments of the Lord and his angels at work examining and arranging events *through* time. They were able to view past, present and future simultaneously, observing the cause and effect relationships between past and future events. The rate of progression through time in that place seemed to be disconnected from the speed of the passage of time in the earthly dimension. Amongst my most significant memories of the return to my body was a sense of astonishment that a period of time lasting only one to two minutes had passed in the ambulance. My sense of the time period in the spiritual realm seemed to me to be in the order of around 20 minutes. It is simply not feasible that the events that occurred could have taken place within a minute or two. The only way I can make any sense of that contradiction is to consider that the rate of the passage of time in that place is not linked or related directly to the passing of time on earth.

This brings to mind the many times in the Bible where God is identified as the God of eternity, the "alpha and omega" (which equates to the A and Z in the English language,) the beginning and the end. He is beyond time! How could the laws of his own creation bind the creator of the universe? God stands *outside* time and can observe and manipulate events *throughout* all time from a position that is *not fixed at any one point* in time. He is the eternal one! I hope you can begin to understand the enormity of his being as you consider this aspect of his nature.

Sensing the way in which Jesus and the angels were able to look forward through time to observe events, choices and outcomes gave me a completely new understanding of the relationship between human decisions and the unfolding of events through time. At one point in the spiritual body when discussing my actions into the future, Jesus instructed the angels to look further into the future to see the outcomes of actions and decisions that would be made on my return to the earthly life. I was able to sense their ability to discern the actions and events that had not yet taken place in my life. They were literally looking into the forthcoming events of my life and I was observing them in the process of evaluating my own future. More than this they were able to warn me that actions I might take would become a risk to my faith at a point in the future.

The best I can offer as a description of that process is to illustrate using a metaphor. When someone is driving in a car it is possible to see forward to a certain extent, partly with natural vision and partly with the predictive assumptions we make about the way our highways are built, signposted and arranged. The point of view available to the angels is more like being in a helicopter flying above that road, giving the pilot a chance to see well beyond the visual range of the driver on the road. The pilot can choose to skip ahead and observe the traffic, obstacles and intersections that are not visible to the car driver, the person within their body on the earthly level.

The angels could see the changes that would be caused by decisions or events that took place in the present, a wrong turn, a rest stop, a flat tire or a decision to speed up or slow down. They can give warnings against making decisions that will lead to disaster. They can give directions for the most direct route to a destination. The angels were able to look forward on the "road map" of my life and observe the route I would be taking through time.

It was also clear that Jesus had ability far beyond that of the angels as he was instructing them to see the eventual outcomes of present life decisions. It seemed that he could almost instantaneously know the future, whereas the angels, operating at a less advanced level, had to read the future. He had instructed them to look forward into my future to confirm a course of events that he was already aware of, but that the angels did not know without intentionally looking forward to observe the future.

Being the subject of this detailed observation, I was naturally intrigued and curious as to the outcomes but was very clearly given a limited view of my future life. I sensed the Lord saying to the angels "He should not see this." I gathered that this was so as not to influence my decision-making when I returned to the physical body. I was then asked to decide in advance concerning my actions on earth when I returned. I was clearly informed that there would be risks for me on a soul level, the implications of making wrong decisions and the benefits of following through with right decisions. The choices I was to make on my return would shape my own future and affect the future of others.

"In him we were also chosen, having been predestined according to the plan of him who works out everything in conformity with the purpose of his will." [Eph. 1:11 NIV]

"We speak of God's secret wisdom, a wisdom that has been hidden and that God destined for our glory before time began." [I Cor 2:7 NIV]

The knowledge of the future that Christ used to foresee events in my life has given me a new understanding of the role of pre-destiny in God's plan for my life and the lives of every human being who has lived. My story has already been written and yet I am within the story, living in its pages, making decisions and choices, judging, forgiving and moving through a complex matrix of time and God-guided destiny. In my earthly mind I make a choice. It is chosen with a free will and yet Christ and the angels were able to observe the choices I had not yet made. My life is not predestined because God dictates my choices, it is predestined because God is above time and already knows the entire story from start to finish and is waiting for us at the end of the timeline.

Our choices effectively sculpt the future. God is looking back at our choices from the future, observing and foreseeing our choices from the past, guiding, advising and influencing our choices in the present. He knows the reasons behind our choices, the motivations that drive them, the circumstances that shape them and the consequences of making those choices. Yes, our choices are made with a free will, but God knows what is within those choices from all angles, past, present and future. Does this contradict the notion of free will? Not at all! Being above time means that inevitably the future is known. It must be, for God, who is above time, cannot see it any other way. It is not possible for God to be who he is and not know all of time.

One of the most devastating impacts of returning to my body and leaving the spiritual realm behind was the loss of this awareness. Moving away from the experience of feeling, of being a part of the process of seeing through time, however small that part was, felt as if I had returned to a prison that limited the enormous overview of time that I had experienced through my communication with the Lord while in the spirit. I felt chained to the moment of "now," whereas I had, for a short moment, been free to observe through Jesus the immense expanse of time and space. That experience was incomparable and indescribable. I am still lost for words to capture the scale and dimensions of that awareness.

I have come to understand now more than ever the role God plays in guiding human destiny via the angels and through the agency of Jesus and the Holy Spirit. History and destinies are written in critical tipping points of decision that initiate or destroy dynasties, alter the course of nations, or even affect the direction of all humanity. The Old Testament is full of incredible moments of decision that led to the creation of and preservation of the nation of Israel. Abraham choosing to listen to God and leave his homeland, Isaac born as a child of promise resulting from Abraham's faith, Jacob swindling the blessing from his dying father, Joseph sold into slavery in Egypt by his brothers to later provide a haven for them in a time of severe famine. Moses discovered by "chance" as a baby floating in the river and being raised in Pharaoh's household. Each of these choices and chances had enormous implications for the instigation and survival of the nation of Israel.

God foresaw that Israel would be the bearers of his teachings and his law. Eventually they would become the source of the great man-God Jesus the chosen one, who would transform human spirituality and introduce a creed of love, forgiveness and equality into a world full of blind legalism, cruelty and hatred. Without these choices and chances concepts such as compassion for the poor, equal rights, universal justice and freedom of choice may not have eventuated in the world we know today.

Does this seem on a far larger scale than the individual who suffered a heart attack and found himself face to face with Jesus and his angels? Yes, but each of the examples mentioned above were individual occurrences of God's intervention into the world we live in. Seeing through the expanse of time enables him to manipulate small events to bring about enormous consequences. God works at the level of small human choices that bring about massive global changes. Through this knowledge and wisdom one man, Jesus, was able to shake the planet and affect it profoundly for millennia to come. One moment of choice and surrender in the garden of Gethsemane transformed all of history and liberated humanity. Surely it is no surprise that Jesus was sweating drops of blood at that time, knowing the enormity of the moment, that the future of all humanity hinged on his simple words, "Not my will, but yours be done." That simple moment of surrender has set free every soul who believes in him and will give rise to an eternal kingdom on earth. One small moment of decision led to enormous consequences for the future.

I should now rein in these expansive thoughts and return to my personal experience or run the risk of digressing into the infinite. In the spirit, the choice that was given me was this; to return to my body and continue my earthly existence, knowing that if I remained with the Lord in the heavens I could live in the bliss and joy of heart I was feeling forevermore, or to return to the physical world and continue my earthly journey. It was made plain to me that my choices would set the path of the future. The future was not written, or indeterminate, but it depended on my decisions, my actions and my words, which would decide the path I would take and the people I would effect on that path. I chose to return, to face the risk and continue in my frail human body to walk the way of mortal life's forking road, doing my best to make the right choices on the path God had laid before me.

Speaking now of the risk of returning it is difficult to communicate the importance of our decisions and actions in the physical world without sounding a little like a fire and brimstone preacher. This much I can say with certainty. As I first became aware that I had left my body and was in the spirit I was confronted with an immense dark void beneath me that filled me with fear. I was also sharply aware of the warmth, love and light that beckoned me toward the heavens. The Lord was very specific in pointing out to me that there was no guarantee that I would return to heaven once I resumed my earthly life. The choices I was yet to make would determine the outcome and those choices are still in motion as long as my life on earth continues.

The choices I had to make on returning to my earthly life were made through hard times, most particularly the death of my daughter Rebekah, whose poor injury racked body was so severely damaged by the car that struck her at the age of seven years, causing massive brain injury and long-term paralysis of nearly all of her body, while leaving her mental functions intact. She succumbed to pneumonia in 2009 and died at the age of 29 years. I grieved her deeply, however the knowledge of a life after death was of immeasurable comfort to me at that time.

There have been several times when I have looked back over the years since my heart attack and heavenly experience with confusion. The woman I had met and married was no longer with me, the risk the Lord had predicted and warned me of had come to pass and I had been put in a difficult position, having to decide on one hand between conformity to cultural acceptance and on the other remaining true to my belief in the cross as the only way to reach unity with God. Deep in my heart I remain confident that I have chosen the right path. I wish I could say that everything had gone perfectly since my return, but that is not the case. Life has been a mixture of wonderful times and great sadness.

Through it all, however, I can see that God has a purpose and a plan in my life to spread the word of my experience and be a witness of the existence of heaven, of a living Christ, and the hope of an eternal future. I continue to share this knowledge with as many people as I possibly can, and I know that God has his hand on me every time I write or speak of these events, now and forever. Without him I am nothing. I go on in the belief that some lives will be changed through the telling of this story, that his great love will emerge from the pages and transform hearts and souls.

My experience has enabled me to understand that time is a temporary state and that we are destined, if we believe in him, to move beyond the earthly limitations that hold us back. So much more is possible, there are many mountains to climb and lives to transform. I believe this to be the beginning of a journey that will never end. Doubt and confusion are the enemies of faith and I foresee an eventual outcome that will leave this world awestruck and changed forever. In the face of doubt and cynicism, the God I experienced remains as a beacon of hope and inspiration.

"Faith is the confidence that what we hope for will actually happen; it gives us assurance about things we cannot see." [Hebrews 11:1 NLT]

# Chapter 4

## Two Worlds

Floating freely in the spiritual body without any physical ties, no nervous system or mental processes clouding the workings of an unaffected soul I was able to look on my life from a very different perspective. The removal of all worldly connection to the body and the unseen spiritual influences that are constantly at work in the earthly dimension oppressing and limiting our spiritual effectiveness, opened my awareness to just how much a soul experiences on the heavenly plane. It is an entirely different ball game. Put simply, the rules are not the same.

In the presence of such perfection I found myself profoundly aware of my own shortcomings. It felt as if every angry moment, violent thought, promiscuous imagination or selfish motive had attached itself to me in the form of a stain or a rip in the fabric of my soul. I have been a committed Christian for most of my life, with a deep belief that I am forgiven of my sins. I still do not in any way question that belief. I do however understand more fully that all existence on our earthly plane is deeply flawed and that the residue of the physical life clings to our soul even when we are removed from our body.

"All of us have become like one who is unclean and all our righteous acts are like filthy rags; we all shrivel up like a leaf and like the wind our sins sweep us away." [Isaiah 64:6 NIV]

Face to face with a perfect being, surrounded by angels of light and immersed in an ocean of love, my own humanity became like a stinking odor to me. I longed to shed the skin of the past, the associated earthly imperfections and to shine in purity as the angels did. I felt the love of God glowing within me, overwhelming me with the generosity of his willingness to allow a flawed, desperate soul such as mine to be in his presence.

Caught between these two contradictory worlds that conflicted my very deepest inner being I came to the most complete understanding of God's grace that I have ever experienced. Yet why did I continue to feel impure if my sins were forgiven?

The revelation I received was this; our sins are *pardoned* through our unity with Jesus. This does not mean they do not exist, but that in the heavens we are not held responsible for them. They are removed from us as far as the East is from the West [Psalm 103:12]. Christians are given a promise that clearly states that we are not *liable* for our sin, that the stains of imperfection will be washed away from us when we enter the heavenly dimension and when we leave our physical existence behind us. This is a concept that is repeated throughout the pages of the New Testament:

"He anointed us, set his seal of ownership on us and put his spirit in our hearts as a deposit, guaranteeing what is to come" [II Cor 1:21-22 NIV]

"So it will be with the resurrection of the dead. The body that is sown is perishable, it is raised imperishable; it is sown in dishonor, it is raised in glory; it is sown in weakness, it is raised in power; it is sown a natural body, it is raised a spiritual body." [I Cor 15:42-44 NIV]

The fulfillment of the Christian covenant occurs in the spiritual body. What we have while in the physical body is a contract with God that our human imperfections will not be held against us when we ascend to the heavens. We are forgiven now in advance of a judgment process that will occur in the future, or after our death. What we have available to us now is a ticket of entry, a passport or a visa to enter the kingdom of heaven. I experienced this knowledge at the deepest level. I felt the process at work, the conflict of physical residue with heavenly perfection. I felt the overpowering generosity of love ready to erase and separate me from the dirt that clung to my spiritual self.

This same process was experienced by several of the prophets of the Bible. Isaiah and John were both purified of this earthly imperfection when they found themselves in the Heavenly realm. [Isaiah 6:5-6 Rev.1:17] God seems always to encourage humans who find themselves in the presence of the divine, telling them not to fear and helping them to stand in his presence and offering them a means of purification from the earthy existence. God is clearly calling humanity to transcend the guilt and uncleanness of this realm and to rise into the realm of the heavenly kingdom without fear.

If any reader begins to speculate as to whether this imperfection or allegorical staining of the soul was perhaps reserved for me as an individual as a result my own unique individual sins and that others who had lived a better life perhaps would not experience this uncleanness in the presence of God, I would remind them that even the prophets, disciples and great men of God found themselves trembling with the weight of their personal guilt when found in the heavens. This is a universal and common human condition.

Standing in the presence of the angels of God offered me a reference point from which to observe the human condition. It was the experience of standing in the presence of perfection that revealed to me the full extent of the imperfection that is integral to human life. We live on this earth locked in a cycle of decay and surrounded by spiritual forces that bind us and lead us away from the light of heavenly purity. When confronted with the reality of this clearly evident contrast, the foolishness of our human reluctance to pursue the path of light was a painful realization that reduced me to a desperately apologetic state. Standing in the presence of angels it is all so clear, so obvious and simple to understand and yet here in the physical body it remains veiled and hidden from our understanding.

Many readers who have not experienced a Christian rebirth of the soul could easily label this chapter as a sanctimonious lecture from a Christian on repentance. This could not be further from the truth of my experience, or my motivation. Having been there and felt firsthand the impurity of my humanity and seen the amazing purity and love of Christ and the angels, I could not return here to earth with a clear conscience if I did not share the power of that experience openly with any who are willing to listen. This is urgent, this is a life and death decision! This will affect your existence for all eternity! Once you have died and found that you continue to exist in a spiritual state the rules change profoundly.

It is easy to dismiss the concept of repentance as an old-fashioned fire and brimstone preacher's weapon of fear and intimidation, offered as a means of escaping the burning flames of hell. Having stood on the threshold and experienced the heavenly light, if only in a limited way, I am confident that the greatest fear that we human souls can have is the threat of missing out on the incredible love, joy and completion that can be found in paradise. If I am to preach on the meaning of repentance it will be to say that the importance of repentance is to gain access to the most magnificent existence any person can imagine. This is a simple change of emphasis, but a significant one. Rather than the big stick of punishment, I believe in a powerful, liberating freedom to ascend into the heights of a purely spiritual existence. Repent and be saved in order to receive a VIP pass to the greatest destination you could ever dream of or imagine.

To repent is defined as feeling such great regret for past conduct as to change one's mind regarding it. You may be asking yourself why I am laboring the point of repentance so heavily. It is difficult to communicate the importance of this matter in words alone. To walk this world, to exist in this body, to be a soul assigned to a physical vessel carries with it an innate contradiction. This contradiction can only be totally comprehended when the soul is freed from the ties and influences, attractions and attachments of the physical world. As an unattached soul the physical existence seems heavy, clumsy, restrictive and tainted. Just to exist and function in the body is a burden to the soul, which is naturally drawn to the light and unrestricted freedom of heaven.

Repentance is the physical expression of the heavenly order in the earthly life. To be sorry for the way I have lived, the trouble and strife I have caused, the damage I have inflicted on other souls and to wish to change that behavior from selfish acts of pride and greed into acts of love, truth and joy, is in a very real sense the invasion of the earth by the heavens. Our willingness to bring love into existence is creating the kingdom of heaven within the lower dimensions of earth. "Thy kingdom come, thy will be done on earth as it is in heaven," can be directly equated to the great command, "Love thy neighbor as thyself."

Each of us is a portal to another dimension, in which the contrast of good and evil is evident in this world as acts of love or hate. We express heaven on earth when we love other people. My experience of heaven was the purest and most complete sense of love imaginable. Bringing just a small taste of that love into this world is like opening a small window to heaven and letting a little breeze from that blessed place blow into the stale, putrid air of this prison cell existence.

Prior to my death experience and even more so since that time, I have had an ever increasing sense that there is so much more for us to know and that the mysteries of the Bible, of God and of our experience of heaven and earth, are only partly understood in our present forms of worship and church life. After returning to this life I prayed to be shown more of God, to know more of his way of working in this earth and to have his mysteries revealed to me in a deeper sense than I had encountered before. I had been taken to such depths of emotion, love and communication while in the heavens that I did not feel my church experience adequately reflected the power, beauty and truth I had encountered in the spiritual realm.

Through various means, partly coincidental encounters, some past and some present experience and the tireless searching for a deeper knowledge of God, I was led to an encounter with several ancient Hebrew texts. There is a body of knowledge it is claimed, which is the oral tradition of Judaism passed from generation to generation since the time of Abraham down until the present day. Although the teachings have been altered and exaggerated over the centuries, I believe God has led me to explore this ancient knowledge as an answer to my prayers. The Pharisees and Rabbis of the first century were also teachers of an exclusive knowledge of these oral traditions and I believe it was Jesus willingness to spread the teachings so freely that was one of the major reasons they hated him to the point of having him killed. The secrecy at that time was particularly stringent and Jesus appeared to be offering it to the simple people of his time, while the Pharisees were teaching an elitist restriction of the knowledge of the Kingdom:

"Woe to you, teachers of the law and Pharisees, you hypocrites! You shut the door of the Kingdom of Heaven in people's faces. You yourselves do not enter, nor will you let those enter who are trying to." [Matt. 23:13 NIV]

Enough to say that there is more to the prophetic visions of Jacob, Joseph, Ezekiel and Elijah that we can learn by participating in God's kingdom with our full being, not just our intellect. The experience of another dimension in which good and evil were far more distinct and separate, that was filled with love and in which I encountered the presence of Christ, can be heard clearly reflected in a couple of very significant writings that I consider to be directly linked. The first of these is in the letter of Paul to the Romans, in which he says;

"For I am convinced that neither death nor life, neither angels nor demons, neither the present nor the future, nor any powers, neither height nor depth, nor anything else in all creation, will be able to separate us from the love of God that is in Christ Jesus our Lord." [Romans 8:38-39 NIV]

The Sefir Yetzirah, one of the foundation texts of the ancient Hebrew faith, with an opening few chapters that are claimed to have been written by Abraham, also lists a number of similar dimensions.

"A depth of beginning, a depth of end, a depth of good, a depth of evil, a depth of above, a depth of below, a depth of East a depth of West, a depth of North, a depth of South, The singular master, God faithful king dominates over them all from his holy dwelling until eternity of eternities." [Sefir Yetzirah 1:5]

There does appear to be direct correlation between Paul's writing and this document. Why does Paul use this list of dimensions as a summary of the entire universe, quoted as a complete list of the powers and influences that might threaten to separate us from the love of Christ? Surely this is Paul's expression of his understanding of the entirety of creation, the totality of the universe, in which nothing could come between us and the love of Jesus.

Paul studied under the great scholar Gamaliel [Acts 22:3] and was trained thoroughly, "taught according to the perfect manner of the law of the fathers." I believe Paul was trained in the oral tradition and was familiar with the words written in the Sefir Yetzirah. I believe the Lord has led me to this body of knowledge to help bring us to a greater understanding of the context in which Jesus taught and Paul preached. I also believe we Christians have a lot to learn from this Jewish tradition, although in its traditional Hebraic form it lacks the true knowledge of Jesus as the Messiah. Paul, however, certainly did not lack that knowledge.

This list of dimensions, or depths, expresses perfectly the immensity of the forces at work in the heavens. The depth of past and future, or beginning and ending, and the depth of good and evil are dimensions overlaid above the three physical dimensions we are familiar with here on earth. These depths, or dimensions, contain the whole of creation. As we move beyond the limiting factors of time, and of evil, we can enter a freedom of spirit that reveals to us the nature of God. Each of these factors is in a very real sense a limiting force on our understanding of the love of Christ. Time acts to limit us by bringing about anxious thought for tomorrow. Evil holds us apart from God, keeping us away from his presence, a gap that can only be closed by the blood of Jesus cleansing us from guilt. The love of Christ has not been prevented from reaching us despite the universal forces that would hold us away from God.

I believe that the love of Christ is the most powerful force in the universe and that was indeed my experience as I stood in his presence. Time is in his hands. Evil is under his dominion and his power overcomes past, present, future, evil, death and every other force in existence. Paul was expressing an ascending hierarchy of powers and authorities that are subject to the all-conquering power of Jesus as he rides the ancient skies. I can now be a witness to the certain existence of these powers as they exist beyond the physical universe, the hierarchy of the heavens, the presence of angels we do not see, the power of Jesus as an all pervasive force that is unstoppable for those who have ears to hear and eyes to see.

Those ears and eyes are of the spirit, that once open, will bring the kingdom of heaven through the dimensions of the heavens and into the earthly plane. We are the vessels that contain the kingdom of God and it is up to us to explore, to pray, to implore the Lord to teach us more about opening the windows of heaven and bringing heaven to earth. I pray that your ears and eyes are opened as you read the words of this book and that your heart is alight with excitement as the truth of God's magnificent power and love flows through all time and space to overcome the powers and authorities that would stand between us and God.

When referring to the ancient Hebrew writings I am not in any way suggesting that they should be accepted on an equal standing with the Bible. The books of the Bible are a complete and divinely ordained collection of writings inspired by the Holy Spirit that contain all that humanity needs to achieve unity with God and the reward of eternal life with Him. I do however believe that the church is now at a point where we need to understand the way in which the first century church practiced and lived their belief, in their prayer life, their expectation of God to work miracles and their ability to function in the spiritual realm.

If the oral teaching that accompanied the written scriptures of the Old Testament provides a deeper understanding of the mystery of Christ then I am keen to explore that possibility. If there is any conflict with the Word of God in the Bible, I will never give other documents priority over the Word of God.

The research I have done to date suggests to me that Jesus and the first century believers were not only familiar with these oral traditions, but that Jesus offered a new, controversial and more complete understanding of the ancient mysteries and that his teaching took the mystery from the exclusive domain of the scribes, pharisees and teachers of the law and made it available to the poor and simple people who had previously been denied this knowledge. Jesus' claim to be the one who completed the law and the prophets indicates a belief structure that encompassed all of the previous teachings of Judaism and took them to a higher level, as the divine incarnation of the Godhead, as man and messiah would have been expected to achieve. Jesus integrated all that Moses, David and the School of the Prophets had taught and added his own divine awareness and direct connection with the Father to create a new and more complete path to God known in the first century as "the way." (See Acts 19:23).

The church is now entering a spiritual place and a time where the gifts of the Holy Spirit are powerfully emerging in the faith life of God's people. Healing, prophecy and other miraculous gifts are becoming a regular occurrence in the practice of Christianity worldwide. The books of Bill Johnson, among many others, bear witness to many supernatural works of God and it seems that this emergence of God's Holy Spirit is gathering momentum. We are on the threshold of a new era of Christianity that is not imprisoned by the traditions of men practicing religious rituals, but brings believers into direct contact with the face of Jesus himself, enabling us to hear his voice directly and come into his presence through the power and freedom of his Holy Spirit. It is in the Holy Spirit and in the close connection I have experienced with the Lord that I am now prompted by God to share with you a new level of prayer, visualization and connection with him in the heavens.

My experience of being in the presence of the Lord has seen me re- enter this life with a renewed determination to discover the fullness of the teaching of Jesus and the guidance of the Holy Spirit, to know how to put his words into practice and to live in a closer connection with him on a daily basis. This has required being willing to step out in faith and go beyond the customary forms of worship that have become somewhat of a "comfort zone" for the church.

This next phase of growth that God is revealing in and through the church will involve moving beyond the safe zone and allowing the power of God to flow from heaven into the earth through his followers. The power of God is not inaccessible but is readily available to those who are willing to live in faith, as Paul the Apostle says:

"Do not say in your heart, 'Who will ascend into Heaven?'" (that is, to bring Christ down) "or 'Who will descend into the deep?'" (that is, to bring Christ up from the dead). But what does it say? "The word is near you; it is in your mouth and in your heart," that is, the message concerning faith that we proclaim. [Romans 10: 6-8 NIV].

Paul is here requiring us to believe *into* the heavens that Jesus is alive there, to believe *through* death that Jesus has emerged from the grave and also to declare that as Christians we are not limited by those barriers We can overcome them through belief, through the declaration of our words that bring the power of heaven to earth and that bring us from death into eternal life with him.

"For it is with your heart that you believe and are justified and it is with your mouth that you profess your faith and are saved. As Scripture says, "Anyone who believes in him will never be put to shame." [Romans 10:10-11 NIV]

The mystery of Christ will demand that we are willing to step out of our familiar earthly existence and into a kingdom beyond death with Christ in the heavens. And yes, the mystery of Christ will take you beyond your physical body and into your spiritual body, out of this world and into the realm of the angels, out of this finite time and into eternity, out of the world as we know it and into the kingdom of heaven on earth. The mystery of Christ is the belief and awareness that we as human beings can and will go beyond the barriers of the physical world and bring the kingdom of God to earth. And where do we gain access to this kingdom?

Remember the words Jesus spoke while on earth: "The kingdom of God is within you." [Luke 17:21 KJV]

The mystery of Christ is to learn to ascend the ladder to the Heavens and to descend again to earth with the kingdom of God alive within you. The only barrier that can prevent this is unbelief. Our faith will allow us to declare heavenly things on earth, to overcome hatred with love, to overcome death with life, to overcome fear with joy, to be in the presence of our Lord and to know the voice of our master. This book is a call to all readers to be brave enough to take the next step of faith. We can be in the presence of Jesus Christ in the heavenly kingdom if we believe it is possible, seek within ourselves for the kingdom of God and "enter his gates with thanksgiving and his courts with praise." [Psalm 100:4 NIV] These gates are a spiritual symbol for entry into the heavenly Zion, the kingdom that exists both in heaven and within us. Yes, the gates to his kingdom are within you.

# Chapter 5

## Within the Temple Within

Returning from the Heavens in the spiritual body back to the earth and the physical body brought with it some enormous contradictions and required some significant decisions. Initially I found myself in a rather damaged body with a heart that needed repair in more than one sense. I was suffering from the blockage that had occurred in my heart artery, but was also emotionally damaged by the many years of grief over my beautiful daughter, locked in a body that would not function, bound in a wheelchair with a wonderfully active mind that could barely express itself through the minimal movements and limited vocal sounds she was capable of making. I was desperately in need of restoration.

In the first chapter of this book I mentioned the way that heaven seemed to follow me back into the hospital, how I was aware of God's presence, of Jesus, of angels and how I returned with a sense of a destiny that I needed to fulfill in my life on earth. Re-entering the world also brought with it the harsh realization that I was back in the battle that is human life. The crushing weight of my physical existence was also reflected in the weight of earthly concerns; my responsibility to provide for my children, to pay the mortgage, the bills and to continue in my career as a lecturer in an undergraduate degree course I was delivering. I was also in the process of finding my place in the world after the separation and divorce I had been through a couple of years beforehand. I was already feeling rather dislocated and separate from the world prior to the heaven experience and now that I had been out of my body and into the spiritual I felt even more isolated and alone, truly a foreigner to this world and this life.

My initial dilemma was to decide whom I would tell of my experience. You may think that this would be obvious, that you would simply blurt it out to everyone you met and that they would accept it with joy and amazement, celebrating the magnificence of the occasion with you. The reality of the situation was somewhat harsher than that. People bring many preconceived beliefs and ideas to the table when you boldly announce your near death experience and return to the world. Even more so when you share that you met with the Lord and have spoken with him and the angels. The reactions vary from outright rejection, cynical reservation, interested but not convinced, avoiding you in future because you are obviously mentally unstable, or just "Thanks for telling me that must have been amazing," with no further interest. These responses along with concerns about my credibility as an educator and the fact that one month after the experience I was asked to take on a leadership role in my place of work, led me to be reserved and cautious about who I shared the experience with.

On the other hand there was a continuing excitement and amazement at how I was continually placed alongside people who desperately needed to hear this message. Those who had lost people close to them, those who had loved ones who were terminally ill and even more incredibly, those who were about to lose people but did not know that it was going to happen. On more than one occasion I was able to share my experience with people who soon after had a death in the family and were greatly comforted by hearing my account before the death had occurred. I am in no doubt whatsoever that the Lord had his hand on every chance meeting, every spontaneous conversation and discussion of life after death that I have engaged in since that time.

I was torn between the earthly concerns of career, respectability and credibility on one hand and the burning need to tell the world about the life after death experience and the greatness of God on the other. I was also working hard to restore my heart and body to good working order and had to build up my physical strength from a very low point to be able to function effectively in the world.

The question I have asked myself and I would not be surprised if you, the reader, have asked the same question, is why I have waited for so many years to record and publish this account of the events. Several things combined to throw me off course with this intended path. The minister of my church, while interested, was in some doubt of my experience, as he did not feel it fitted the pattern of other Christian accounts of life after death experiences. This concerned me greatly and was a great disincentive for me to proceed further with speaking about it within my church. Thankfully the Lord did speak to me through one of the other church ministers, briefly but specifically confirming to me that it was indeed he, Jesus that I had met within the heavens.

It felt as if the earthly forces of reason, logic and doubt were arrayed against me, while the heavenly forces of faith, belief and hope were aligned with me. I was caught in the middle of a personal battle in which doubt would prevent me from spreading the word, but faith would have me shout it from the mountaintop.

Another factor in my delaying the book was that the way I remember the events in the spiritual realm are not the same as memories I have of other events from my earthly life. Memories generated in my physical body originate from the data gathered from the five physical senses. These memories clearly were a record of something very different. These memories were very closely tied to emotions and were more of an awareness of my heart and soul than a record of audio-visual input. It still feels to this day as if I can go back into the memories of those events and feel the connection, the love and the different mode of perception that occurred in the spiritual body. I felt the events with emotion, communication and love rather than being aware of seeing, touching or hearing.

It took time for me to come to understand many of the things that happened to me in the spirit and I now believe that I needed time to learn how to digest the experience in a different way. This was not thought as I had come to know it and yet it was not an experience entirely foreign to my earthly life. The mental and physical elements of what I so lightly refer to as my "self" were removed from the spiritual and emotional parts of my being. This was a new and different existence and yet it remains as much a part of me now as it did in the spiritual realm. The difference is that I am now swamped with physical sensory input, mental activity and the "busy- ness" of life. I still to this moment yearn for the peaceful tranquility and love of that place, to quiet the inner chatter that seems to want to provide a commentary on every occurrence in my life and to draw me into a mental debate over every detail of this earthly existence.

Beneath the hyperactivity of the mind there is a quiet place, a "still small voice" that calls us to come away from the rat race of life on earth and to simply become aware of our existence as a spirit and to know the presence of the Spirit of God within us. Although we consider ourselves to exist as a mind and a body, we are also made up of heart and soul. It is the part of ourselves that we think of as a heart and soul that provided a continuum beyond the barrier of death. *To discover your heart and soul is to know the eternal part of your being.* It is to touch and feel the kingdom of God within you. It is to open a doorway to the eternal pathway to heaven and to open the way for heaven to come into the earth through you.

Some may be concerned that this is just another call to engage in Eastern meditation techniques. Nothing could be further from the truth. To still the mind is not to prevent all thoughts and experiences. It is to close down the noisy machinery that is concerned only with our physical existence and become aware of the Spirit, to know and to experience the presence of Jesus within you. "Be still and know that I am God." [Psalm 46:10 NLT]

To quiet yourself is to open the way to God, to allow him the time and space to fill you with awareness of him and to bask in his amazing presence. Yes, this does require coming away from the hectic demands of life and focusing entirely on feeling and hearing God within you. It is in these moments when I can find peace, quieten the mental chatter and feel God's presence that I experience the same love and joy that pervades the Heavens.

How obvious this is to Christians and yet how rare are the times we manage to practice this simple principle. Jesus instructed his disciples to come away from the crowds and be in prayer, to go into the inner chamber and commune with God. It is this private intimacy with God that enables the kingdom of heaven to manifest within you, that opens the doorway for Jesus to come within you and make his home there and to open a doorway from heaven to earth in your life.

The growing awareness that the sensations and spirituality I had experienced in the heavens were achievable from this earthly life became a powerful driving force in my life. As the months and years rolled on after the heart attack I was drawn ever more powerfully to find ways to reconnect with the Lord in the way I had experienced him in person. I am not talking about conventional Christian prayer, although I do pray regularly and believe implicitly in prayer as the primary means of communication with God. The connection I was seeking was the feeling of being in the presence of Jesus himself, of having his divine mind opened to me, of the overwhelming sense of love and compassion and the inner knowledge that he is in a very literal sense alive within me.

Often it is the simplest of acts that can start you on the path to God. I simply asked him to show me the way to come fully into his presence, to reveal the way to me. Interesting changes began to occur in my bible reading sessions. Certain verses, particularly in the Psalms began to almost leap out of the page at me.

"Enter his gates with thanksgiving and his courts with praise; give thanks to him and praise his name." [Psalm 100:4 NIV]

"Who may ascend the mountain of the LORD? Who may stand in his holy place?" [Psalm 24:3 NIV]

"Lift up your heads, you gates; lift them up, you ancient doors, that the King of glory may come in." [Psalm 24:9 NIV]

"Within your temple, O God, we meditate on your unfailing love." [Psalm 48:9 NIV]

"I rejoiced with those who said to me, "Let us go to the house of the LORD. Our feet are standing in your gates, Jerusalem." [Psalm 122:1-2 NIV]

Why were these verses standing out to me so clearly? I felt that God was calling me to enter the Holy city and ascend to the court of the Temple. I had always understood the metaphorical and symbolic meaning of the Temple, the division of the levels of ascension to God through the courtyard, the Holy Place and the Most Holy Place in the Temple of Solomon, as in the tabernacle before it. The role of the Temple began to be prominent in my thoughts. Why was God bringing this to the center of my awareness and what was he instructing me to do?

My attention was then drawn to the detailed plan of the Heavenly temple as seen by the prophet Ezekiel in his vision (Ezekiel 40-44). Questions were running through my mind. Why such a detailed plan? This was a temple in the heavens, not an earthly building that he saw. Ezekiel had journeyed to the temple in the spirit and was given a guided architectural tour by an angel.

I was then shown the verse in which Paul states clearly that we as believers are the temple of God:

"Don't you know that you yourselves are God's temple and that God's Spirit dwells in your midst? If anyone destroys God's temple, God will destroy that person; for God's temple is sacred and you together are that temple." [I Corinthians 3:16-17 NIV]

And then Jesus identifying the temple as the temple of his body:

"The Jews then said, 'It took forty-six years to build this temple and will you raise it up in three days?' But He was speaking of the temple of His body." [John 2:21 ESV]

And then the author of the book of Hebrews talking of Jesus being our forerunner into the inner sanctuary of the temple:

"We have this hope as an anchor for the soul, firm and secure. It enters the inner sanctuary behind the curtain, where our forerunner, Jesus, has entered on our behalf. He has become a high priest forever, in the order of Melchizedek." [Hebrews 6:19-20 NIV]

I began at last to understand what the Lord was revealing to me.

1. The temple is a way to ascend to God.
2. It is within us.
3. Each level we ascend brings us closer to God.
4. Jesus embodies the way to ascend.

Jesus stated; "Very truly I tell you, you will see 'Heaven open and the angels of God ascending and descending on' the Son of Man." [John 1:51 NIV]

But how could I access this Heavenly temple within? God began to whisper into my heart that to enter a spiritual temple I would have to be in the spirit. I began to search the bible for references to this concept and soon came to the realization that the early church was well familiar with the experience of being in the spirit and being shown visions while in that state. There are also records of the early Christians being taken into the heavens, experiencing communication directly with God and his angels and of meeting with Jesus himself.

"God is spirit and his worshipers must worship in the Spirit and in truth." [John 4:24 NIV]

"Peter knocked at the outer entrance and a servant named Rhoda came to answer the door. When she recognized Peter's voice, she was so overjoyed she ran back without opening it and exclaimed, "Peter is at the door!" "You're out of your mind," they told her. When she kept insisting that it was so, they said, "It must be his angel." [Spirit] But Peter kept on knocking and when they opened the door and saw him, they were astonished." [Acts 12:13-16 NIV]

"On the Lord's Day I was in the Spirit and I heard behind me a loud voice like a trumpet." [Revelation 1:10 NIV]

"For though I am absent from you in body, I am present with you in spirit and delight to see how disciplined you are and how firm your faith in Christ is." [Colossians 2:5 NIV]

God was relentlessly leading me to understand that we all have an existence as a spirit that is not tied to our physical being and that we could access the heavenly temple within ourselves through the spirit. The more I thought about this, the more I found in the ancient Christian faith to support the idea that Jesus provides us with a way to access God in the spiritual realms by taking us through the symbolic layers and divisions of the temple. When Jesus died the curtain that separated the Holy Place from the Most Holy Place was torn from top to bottom, opening the way for us into the inner sanctuary. The book of Hebrews tells us of the new access to the Most Holy Place which has been opened to the believers in Christ and the role he plays in bringing us into the presence of God:

"But when Christ came as high priest of the good things that are now already here, he went through the greater and more perfect tabernacle that is not made with human hands, that is to say, is not a part of this creation. He did not enter by means of the blood of goats and calves; but he entered the Most Holy Place once for all by his own blood, thus obtaining eternal redemption." [Hebrews 9:11-12 NIV]

"Therefore, brothers and sisters, since we have confidence to enter the Most Holy Place by the blood of Jesus, by a new and living way opened for us through the curtain, that is, his body and since we have a great priest over the house of God, let us draw near to God with a sincere heart and with the full assurance that faith brings, having our hearts sprinkled to cleanse us from a guilty conscience and having our bodies washed with pure water." [Hebrews 10:19-22 NIV]

At last I was starting to understand that he was leading me to go within, find the spirit man inside me and enter the temple of God's presence from that place. I began to understand that many of the Psalms were written as allegorical instructions to find the path to God through prayer and meditation on the words of the book. Meditating on the words can help us to understand them in a different way, to open our perception to higher levels of understanding that offer a more complete connection with God.

Then I began to close my eyes, open my spiritual eyes and finally see and understand in the spirit. The first layer of this transition is a change from the images we see physically into the images of "vision." These are the images that dreams are made of. I began to walk in the spirit, along a path up a steep hill to the gates of the City of God, Zion and enter the narrow streets of the city.

# PART TWO

## MEMORY

# Introduction to Part Two

In this part of the book I return to the life I had led prior to my heart attack. The context of my prior life was significant in the struggles I had undergone, the many years of surviving circumstances that were threatening to my faith and my life. I absolutely believe that the events of our lives are intricately woven together and that God knows every strand of that fabric. Dark forces at work trying to destroy me were in conflict with the life-giving power of Christ as he led me through the valley of the shadow of death.

It is inevitable that in telling this story I will refer regularly to the events that occurred in the presence of the Lord, these passages serve the purpose of re-examining the events in light of the experiences that preceded them. As I discussed in Chapter 3 there is no doubt in my mind that time for the heavenly beings is a flexible dimension, through which they can freely gaze and observe the past, present and future. It is reasonable then, to assume that forces of good and evil are battling over our souls through the fabric of time and that events prior to my death experience are directly related to the experience itself and also the events to follow, most particularly the writing of this book. Satan's attempts to destroy Christ, to prevent his kingdom from occurring ahead of time demonstrate both the malicious intent of the forces of darkness to prevent the light from emerging and also their inability to predict the actions of God who can always overcome those attempts. So often it is the very attempts by evil to destroy the light that bring the light into its completeness and perfection. The act of crucifying Jesus has provided the world with a hope for eternal life. In a much smaller, but similar way, it was the very difficulties and tragedies that the Devil threw in my path that gave me the strength and resilience to see the Lord at work throughout tragic life events.

Part two is written to highlight the gleaming thread of God's love that has run through my life, despite my own inadequacies. He is a God who would not let me die, who followed behind me picking up the pieces and putting me back on my feet with every stumble. The memories of life prior to meeting him have established within me an awareness of his omnipresent love, tireless faithfulness and infinite patience. Through it all there remains a strong sense that our times are in his hands, past, present and future and that no weapon of the enemy turned against God's people will fulfill its purpose. I am eternally grateful for his intervention in my life that enabled me to understand and cope with the passing of my daughter, the pain and emotional suffering that I endured and the knowledge that Jesus stood beside me throughout all of those circumstances.

Memory is all that is left of the events I will now recount to you. Memories of pain that have now been diminished by the knowledge that even death cannot hold us down or keep us from his love. It has been my experience that death was a release from prison and a blessed union with the God that created us. Memory provides me with the template by which I can measure my life and see the unmistakable fingerprints of God as he guided me through the maze of deception and despair, providing me with hope and love even in the darkest moments.

# Chapter 6

## Through the Valley

The long-term effect of experiencing the presence of the Lord at such close quarters was indeed profound. Having passed through the most dangerous times of my recovery I found that my mind was led to consider the past and the journey I had travelled to reach this point in my newly restored life. It was only natural that I would consider my life, in all the detail of its adventures, misadventures, failures, successes, victories, and moments of joy and despair. This was a perfect time to reflect on a life so nearly cut off, but now transformed into a bright new start. I will share a few of the more significant moments that shaped the direction of my life prior to the events described in part one of this book.

It is fair to say that I had not arrived at a close relationship with God without substantial pain and suffering over many years. It is also fair to say that I am by no means an average Christian man, (if there is such a thing). I had experienced an extreme series of events and challenges throughout my life, largely due to my own bad decisions, but I also now realize that throughout this time there was a prolonged spiritual battle for my soul. Looking over the years I can see a struggle between the forces of darkness and God's kingdom to have the dominion in my life. I also now recognize that God's love and compassion has been the most powerful force throughout. He has led me in a very literal sense through the valley of the shadow of death and I know that his hand has been on me the entire time despite the many ways in which I have ignored him, disappointed him and turned my back on him. He remained faithful throughout.

I have always felt God's presence in my life and known of his miracle working power. This was passed onto me by a faithful m other who spent many years of my childhood telling me of God's goodness. I was also blessed to have her as a Sunday school teacher as a young child and I clearly remember the way in which she brought the stories of the bible to life for me, particularly the miracles of the Gospels and the ministry of Jesus on earth. There were also events that she saw as miraculous and gave God the glory for bringing his power into our lives and changing our futures. One story I loved to hear was of a time when she was pregnant with my older brother and was in the city shopping. She was boarding a tram and as she grasped the handrail the tram lurched suddenly, dislodging her hand and sending her backwards, in danger of falling into the path of the cars that were rushing past the tram. She felt sure she was about to be crushed under the traffic and was completely off balance as the tram continued to pull away from the stop. She then felt a hand in her back give her a firm push forward and back on to the tram. She turned to thank the generous stranger who had saved her from disaster and found there was nobody there. A man nearby commented on how she had been very lucky to make it safely onto the tram. He had thought she was beyond help and was sure to fall onto the road. My mother believed with all her heart that an angel saved her that day.

One side of my life was full of such wonder and the love of God, but my experience of the world outside my family was certainly less spiritual. I was a child of the 1960s and a teenager in the 1970s and encountered the counter-culture movement that completely swept the Western world over those decades. I grew up loving music, the Beatles, CCR, Pink Floyd, Santana, Jimi Hendrix and became a guitarist, spending many hours teaching myself to play and practicing until the fingers of my left hand were hard and calloused. With my love of rock music came the associated lifestyle, long haired musicians, hippies, parties and the excitement of discovering that I had become an accomplished guitarist. I was surrounded by the psychedelic experimentation that came with that territory and succumbed to the lifestyle of the time.

This drew me away from the church involvement I had enjoyed as a child to some extent and yet I remained faithful to God in my heart and continued to honor him deeply within myself, even though my actions did not always reflect this. I spent many hours reading the more mystical books of the Bible, the Prophets, and Revelation and loved the spiritual power that was communicated in the words spoken directly from God to his human creation. The mystery of God's timeless knowledge of history, of our collective future and yet his ability to know our own individual destinies always held an air of awesome wonder for me. This God could flick a switch in a moment that would not take effect for months, years, or even centuries, knowing all along the results that would be achieved in the end.

After standing in his presence I now understood to some small extent the intricacies of his ability to weave events through time and space. My intrigue with God's interaction with time has never left me and it has helped me to understand the overarching direction he has provided for me on the bumpy road I have travelled in my lifetime.

My path was not an easy one. Married early at the age of twenty to a woman I truly knew little about apart from the fact that she appeared to share my Christian belief, I became a father to a beautiful son and daughter by the time I was twenty two. I adored my two children and could not get enough time to spend with them, sharing stories, playing games and singing songs with them on my guitar. We had settled in Monbulk, a township in the Dandenong Ranges East of Melbourne, which was an area renowned for its natural beauty, forests and wildlife, new age philosophies and clairvoyants. The wandering hippies of the late 1970s were attracted to this melting pot of various brands of spirituality like bees to honey.

I found myself surrounded by friends and acquaintances that were outwardly spiritual, but inwardly corrupt, drug addicted and vehemently opposed to anything Christian. I tried hard to maintain my Christian life amid this atmosphere but was constantly under peer pressure to conform to the alternative lifestyle that prevailed in the area at that time. I was attending Church sporadically but remained committed to the Lord. I was seeking a way to get closer to him and come into closer relationship. Around 1980 I saw a televised Christian Charismatic Conference which was attended by many thousands of Spirit filled believers and for the first time heard the sound of free worship in the Spirit. It was as if the gates of heaven had been thrown open and I was hearing angels singing in divine harmony through the voices of the enraptured believers who worshiped God with all their hearts. There was an element of supernatural power in this worship and the way it was reaching out to me through the television.

I decided then and there that I needed to find that higher level of communication with God for myself. I enquired at the local Anglican Church and a very conservative minister almost begrudgingly admitted that there was a charismatic renewal at the local Anglican Church in Belgrave. I attended a couple of meetings there and was immediately touched by the power and presence of God among the congregation and I was baptized in the Holy Spirit shortly afterward. I was prayed for during the service and after leaving the church on the way home, I felt that I should try out my ability to speak in tongues. The first few sounds that emerged from my mouth were of my own volition, but I very quickly found myself speaking in a language I had never heard before and was not controlling with my own mind.

The power of God in my life at that time was palpable and I shared this amazing miracle with many of my friends, who were obviously quite challenged and dubious about such a spiritual outpouring in my life. The power of God seemed to simply seep into my very bones, as his Spirit took greater hold on my life and I became more committed to his cause. I felt that my eyes had been opened for the first time and I realized that God's miraculous power was a real force in my life, not the stuff of ancient stories and historical church records.

Surrounded as I was by the forces of darkness in that place I now realize that this was a declaration of war, that the enemy felt his territory invaded and that I had become a primary target. My young wife had been joining me on the journey into the Spirit of God, but there were spiritual forces at work that had other ideas. At one point a friend of ours had invited us to a social day at a large old estate in the area and we went along. There were many young people there, with games, conversation and music in the grounds of a large old house. At one point a young man came up to me and began to talk about the presence of God on earth and I began to express my belief in Jesus.

His response challenged me greatly. He said that Jesus was in the past and that the Christ was now on earth in the form of a woman. I upheld the fact that Jesus was very much alive and well and seated at the right hand of the Father, so how could he be here in the form of a woman? He offered to introduce me to the Christ then and there and shortly after I found myself face to face with a woman I later knew to be Anne Hamilton-Byrne, a renowned cult leader in the Dandenong Ranges who was later charged with several crimes after abuse of several children she had "adopted" and was raising to be a "super-race". I stood my ground firmly, informing her that she was deluded in her belief that she was the Christ and thought little more of it, apart from saying to my wife that it was all very weird and that I wanted nothing more to do with it.

My wife had not taken well to my Holy Spirit baptism and was becoming quite opposed. This became very blatantly obvious when I had prayed for her to receive the Holy Spirit and she shortly after broke out in a severe rash over much of her body. She became progressively angrier with me, claiming that the spiritual forces behind speaking in tongues had caused the condition. Not long after this she left me and took up residence with another man, leaving me alone with the children and rarely seeing them. Knowing the characteristics of the Hamilton-Byrne group "the family," I now have little doubt that they brought about the destruction of my marriage. Advice to leave marriages and set up new relationships was commonplace within the group.

This certainly did not fit my vision of the way I had expected God to shape my life. I felt betrayed on many levels, abandoned by God and heart broken. My children were taken from me after spending a short time with my parents and although I was able to see them fortnightly it was never the same close relationship that I had enjoyed with them as a father for the first few years of their lives. In our society fathers are a severely undervalued part of the family structure and the relationship between a young dad and his children was far too easily dismantled. I mourned the separation from my children.

Divorced with two children at the age of twenty four I felt alone in the world, surrounded by a lifestyle I did not respect or understand. The environment in the Dandenong Ranges was not the same easy-going companionship of young musicians and philosophers I had come to enjoy in the 1970s. Something in the atmosphere had changed and I felt threatened by my surroundings. In the middle of my confusion I did not forget Jesus and was calling out to him consistently for guidance and help. Many more of my friends were being caught in the deceptive web of Anne Hamilton-Byrne and several of them suffered mysterious mental breakdowns, which I later discovered were due to the practices of the cult. They believed that large doses of LSD and other such hallucinogenic drugs, mixed with amphetamines and psychiatric drugs such as Sodium Amatol, caused a "going through" to a higher state of consciousness.

From what I observed it did little more than destroy lives, even to the point of suicide in many cases. Their combination of drug taking and mind control techniques proved to be a destructive force and despite their claims to be no more than a harmless spiritual meditation group, they were later revealed to be a group of horrendous predators who sought to take control of people's lives and dominate them with intimidation, threats and oppression.

They continued to aggressively seek followers through a variety of deceptive and coercive tactics for many years and reportedly their movement still exists in the area. I thank God to this day that I saw the deception for what it was and kept apart from this evil and dangerous organization.

I left Melbourne for some time and went on tour with a band as a sound mixer and worked hard as a roadie for some time in an attempt to move beyond the hopeless situation I had found myself in. This was a great experience in some ways, as I found myself working with some significant musicians and really enjoying their company. After six months of relentless touring I finally decided to step out of the music scene, as I was missing my children and I had started a new relationship. By strange coincidence, (or was it?) she was a good friend of the natural mother of Sarah Hamilton-Byrne who had been manipulated into adopting out baby Sarah to the cult. We were married in 1985. I maintained my belief in Jesus throughout this relationship and she also professed a belief in Jesus.

In 1986 I chose to move away from the Dandenong Ranges and shifted to a house down in the outer suburbs of Melbourne and away from the unhealthy atmosphere I had found myself in. I had hoped that this would provide me with a fresh start and for a while we enjoyed the new house and establishing our marriage. I remained very concerned about the upbringing of my children and I was aware that there was a great spiritual danger to them and was constantly praying for their protection.

I began to have a recurring dream. I saw a school pedestrian crossing and one of my children walking across the road. I knew that they would be hit by a car and could not cry out to warn them of the inevitable accident. This dream repeated many times over the period of a year or two and I became convinced that this was God warning me of a real accident. I knew deep within myself that this was a prophetic warning. I told my wife and also expressed my concern to the mother of my children that this could be a warning about the future. She did, rather surprisingly, listen to what I had to say.

December the fifteenth, 1987, was a hot and blustery day in Melbourne, Australia. Searing heat and gusts of wind made it an unpleasant day to be outdoors and the children were thirsty. My children Luke and Rebekah arrived home to find that their mother was not there. Being thirsty and hot they decided to walk to the shop across the road and buy an ice cream to cool them down. On the way home they saw their mother's car pull into the driveway and thinking that they would be scolded for leaving the house they started to run home. Luke, being older and faster, sprinted across the school crossing safely and into the house.

Rebekah was younger, smaller and slower. I do not know the exact sequence of events but can only assume that a gust of wind must have blown Rebekah's long blonde hair across her face at the precise moment she was looking to see if any traffic was approaching. Her view of the oncoming car was blocked, and she ran onto the school crossing. She was struck by the car, thrown into the air and her head impacted with the concrete curb on the side of the road some twenty meters from the place she was hit.

Meanwhile in my house some ten kilometers away, I suddenly became extremely dizzy and said to myself, "This is it! It has happened." About twenty minutes later I received a call telling me that my daughter had been badly injured and that I should go to the hospital immediately. There she lay, seemingly lifeless, a precious little seven year old girl barely breathing and not moving a muscle. The doctors informed us that there was severe trauma to the head and that she would have to be taken to the Royal Children's Hospital in the city, where they had the equipment and expertise to treat that level of injury. And so began a long, long journey of grief, redemption, despair and hope, a battle with the forces of evil and a deepening of my faith, belief and reliance on Jesus as a good and loving God who would guide me through the darkness.

# Chapter 7

## Hope in the Face of Despair

There is nothing that can sap your spirit quite as much as sitting by the bedside of your child not knowing if they will live or die. The medical staff at the Royal Children's Hospital informed me that Rebekah had been badly injured, with a crushed skull and severe internal bleeding on the brain. The prognosis was devastating. They warned us that she would be in a coma for some time and that there was no guarantee that she would ever regain consciousness. They suggested strongly that we should take a non-interventionist approach and switch off all life support.

If you are a parent you can only imagine the dull shock of realization that you were about to lose your child and that the doctors were asking us to decide to end her life rather than prolong her life artificially. I have never felt as conflicted in one moment as at that time, considering the possibility that the Lord may act to heal my daughter and that if I chose to switch off life support I may prevent that possibility. On the other hand, to keep her alive artificially as a shell of a body devoid of any sign of life seemed to me to be a worse option. Several days had gone by and Rebekah had still not moved a muscle. The bleeding had been its worst in the area of the brain stem, which meant the connections between her brain and body via the spinal column had been badly damaged at the base of her brain.

There she lay, my dear seven year old blonde haired blue eyed little angel, breathing slowly but as still as a statue in every other way. We decided to trust in God's will that we would not proceed with life support or a tracheostomy but would leave the situation in God's hands and see whether Bek would make it through. The doctors were urging us that this would be the best course of action as they strongly suspected she would never regain consciousness due to the severity of the injuries to her brain.

Life or death, the cutting edge of existence that tapped into my deepest survival and protective parenting instincts was confronting me for the first time. I prayed like I had never prayed in my life before. The only life support Bek received was a naso-gastric tube into her stomach and a tube inserted into her brain cavity to allow the pressure of swelling to be relieved to avoid further brain damage.

There did come one moment of crisis, when Rebekah's body temperature and heart rate began to drop dramatically. Her pulse rate dropped as low as 45 beats per minute and alarms began to sound loudly, bringing the nurses running from all corners of the Intensive Care Unit. I stood beside her bed, watching the numbers go down and I called out to God for help.

At that moment my wife fainted and fell to the floor next to Rebekah's bed. There I stood, my daughter on the bed dying and my wife unconscious on the floor and I cried out to God with all my heart for assistance, to restore life to my daughter who was obviously slipping away at this stage and asked Him to be with me in the center of the disaster. I called on the name of Jesus and I begged for his power to come into the situation.

I felt a shift in the atmosphere of the room, as if the air had become warmer. Rebekah's pulse rate began to lift and her body temperature began to rise. I had a vivid vision of her looking down on me from above and smiling and then it faded as quickly as it had come. I believe absolutely that God spared her life at that moment. It was as if a cold and dark presence had left the room and had been replaced with a warmth of hope and relief that Rebekah was still with us. This was truly tearing me apart at the deepest core of my being and yet among the uncertainty, fear and emotional torture of the situation I heard God's voice reassuring me, telling me to have faith and go on believing in him.

Days turned into weeks and still Rebekah continued to breathe steadily, not moving so much as an eyelash, lying as still as a corpse. I dreaded that she would remain this way forever. Rebekah had apparently not lost the will to live. She had not simply ceased to breathe, or slipped gently away, but was steadily continuing, persisting and insisting on life in her own silent pilgrimage through the darkness of coma. The endless waiting and hoping for a breakthrough was grueling. I prayed, I fasted and I screamed out to God, asking him why this had happened. I simultaneously resented him for letting this happen, but desperately clung onto him as the only hope I had. Only he had the power over life and death, to raise someone up or to strike them down. I was ready to accept one or the other, but this endless waiting and watching for a flicker of and eyelid or a twitch of a finger seemed to last for an eternity.

Many times I sat with my daughter in the hospital bed, cradling her head on my lap and putting my arms around her chest just to let her know that I loved her. Many times I cried out to God to take me instead and let her live a normal life. I was desperately wounded in the heart.

Eventually there was a flutter of an eyelid, a slight twitch of movement in her fingers and we began to realize that this had not been a coma in the conventional sense, but that all movement had been prevented by the destruction of her brain stem and that we were now seeing the first signs of reconnection as the brain and spinal cord attempted to build new neural pathways to re-establish movement. Very gradually a little movement began to appear in the left hand, the eyes started to open slightly and I heard the first low moans from her mouth. These were the first signs of life I had seen or heard in nearly three months. Gradually signs of awareness began to be visible. A vocal response when asked a question. A twitch of a finger when we conversed with her. The medical staff informed us that the most recovery she would achieve would take place up to 18 months after the injury and that not much improvement would continue after that time frame.

A time of intense effort then commenced, with Rebekah's mother attempting a variety of experimental therapies to stimulate recovery. Being the non- custodial parent, I was only able to see Rebekah fortnightly and this was in itself a form of torment. I received concerning reports from friends of Rebekah being left on the floor on a thin mattress, lying on her front in the hope that she would eventually learn to lift herself with her arms and begin the restoration of movement. I understand that this therapy may be effective in patients with lesser brain injuries, but for Rebekah this was a disaster. She did not regain movement in her right arm, however her left arm became strong. As a result she would constantly push herself up with her left arm, crushing the right side of her chest and gradually deforming her rib cage as she grew over the next two years.

Although I initially tried to assist in the treatment in the hope that there would be a rapid recovery, I soon realized that constantly leaving Rebekah on the floor in the hope that she would restore movement was causing irreparable damage. The structural deformation of her rib cage became alarming in its proportions. I tried on several occasions to persuade Rebekah's mother to cease the treatment and adopt a more conventional medical approach to supporting her spine with a wheelchair specially designed for her condition. She refused and continued with the unorthodox treatment regime. At that stage I decided that legal action was required and I sought to be given custody of my two children.

I had not given up believing for a healing in Rebekah's life and I continued to pray unceasingly for her to be restored to full health. There came a point where I had to accept that we needed to take a responsible course of action and provide her with the treatment regime that would at least give her a chance at maintaining a normal body shape and leading a normal life. It is hard to interact with people when lying on your face on the floor. I knew there was a spiritual battle involved and that the forces of evil were attempting to destroy our lives and our faith in God.

This became particularly evident when the custody proceedings commenced three years after her accident. We were asked by the court to attend a mediation session with a counselor, the counselor being a pastoral worker who was employed by the court to help settle disputes in family law. While waiting for the appointment I distinctly felt an evil presence in the room and my former wife quite spontaneously and without any warning began to curse me loudly. I do not mean that she used bad language. She literally cursed me, my family and my life. I began to pray aloud, not wishing to hear the content of her curses any longer and seeking God's protection. She continued to curse louder, even going as far as far as pronouncing death over me. I continued to pray.

Eventually the counselor interrupted the unusual exchange and called her into the consultation room, shortly followed by me. The mediation session did not achieve much but did reveal to the counselor the nature of the spiritual conflict behind the situation. He had been listening through the closed door and was shocked by the viciousness of her attack. He felt I did have valid reasons for seeking custody and supported my application, recognizing that there was no chance of a mediated outcome given the emotional intensity of the disagreement. Her parents also supported my claim for custody, as they were dismayed at the treatment Rebekah was receiving.

The point of recounting this event is not the legalities of the court case, but to highlight the spiritual attack on me that was to reappear in various forms over the years to come, as Satan began to attempt to destroy my life in a variety of ways. My faith in Jesus was being tested at a far greater level than I had ever thought possible.

The court were not convinced of my arguments for custody, as my first wife denied any mistreatment and maintained that the experimental therapy was a valid approach to Rebekah's recovery. Thankfully the court did not entirely agree and insisted that she be provided with a wheelchair that would offer spinal support and assist her body to be restored to a more normal shape. That was a minor victory and Rebekah soon became more mobile, able to interact at a greater level and eventually began to attend school with an attendant, as she was obviously mentally alert but unable to speak or walk. She could make signs to some extent with her left hand and make verbal sounds that indicated her emotional condition and assent or disagreement.

This may seem like a sizeable detour from the theme of this book and yet I am sure that the sheer heart ache of living through this grief stricken period of my life did have a profound impact on my relationship with God and contributed to the heart trouble I experienced years later. Grief is a heavy burden to bear and hope unfulfilled can sap the spirit of a person over years. Such was my experience.

I had many years of beautiful parenting with my two beautiful daughters Hannah and Evelyn and then was blessed with a young son, James. Underlying this joy was an unrelenting sadness at the ongoing struggle of Rebekah's life. She had become fully aware, but unable to move with any control apart from her face and left arm. Her signing skills improved with the left hand and she could very slowly form simple single words with her mouth, but sentences were to remain unachievable for her. Her voice however, was highly effective at expressing her emotions, anger, humor, laughter and pain.

Added to all this, a dear member of my family who I will not name, resorted to drugs and became violent toward me. I could see the damage that had occurred in this life as a result of Rebekah's accident. Their behavior began to deteriorate and become quite uncontrollable. I was seeing them regularly and they eventually came to live with me. This was a confused young person and I spent many hours trying to restore their belief in God, in life and their self-worth. Although they did stabilize for some time, they eventually became even more heavily involved in drug taking and I was having great difficulty in maintaining their schooling. They would disappear for days at a time and became aggressively opposed to my attempts to help. There seemed to be no end to the attacks on me and my family, as if the Devil was trying to destroy the spirit within me. I now understand that such a close meeting of the Spirit of God with the works of the enemy is bound to have a profound impact on the lives of those involved.

I had great difficulty maintaining my faith in the face of such hostility and there were many times that I felt God had abandoned me. There seemed to be a malicious force pursuing me, trying to break my belief in the protective power of God and his love toward me. In all of this I must emphasize that I was largely to blame for God's silence in my life. I was not living well, immersed in bitterness and sorrow, bowed down in a grief that had not been dealt with emotionally or spiritually. I can only begin to express the extent of that grief in words, to see my daughter's body racked in pain, deforming as she continued to grow through her adolescent years, unable to hear her words or to know her pent up emotions and frustration that would burst out of her in loud groans, weeping, laughter and desperate attempts to communicate. This was a totally soul-destroying experience for me, for her and for our family.

In the middle of this ongoing torment I continued to call out to God, trusting that there would be some light at the end of the tunnel. I had returned to University in 1991 to study media and English Linguistics in an attempt to secure more reliable employment.

As I have mentioned the member of my family who had become embittered and aggressive had decided to live with me for a few years. After a time my wife reached the end of her endurance as it placed increased pressure on an already stressful marriage situation. She took my two young daughters with her and moved to the country for a few months. This person remained completely uncontrollable and continued to disappear for days on end, reappearing at three or four in the morning. They would appear in my bedroom in an angry and aggressive state of mind, spouting words of hatred and intimidation toward me and on a few occasions threatening my life, holding a knife to my throat. I later found out that they had been keeping company with some of the

Hamilton-Byrne children, now grown to adulthood and still living in the Dandenong Ranges nearby.

Separate from my younger children and my wife, left with an uncontrollable and drug affected adolescent to care for, I felt that my life had truly reached the lowest point possible. I must admit that at this point I virtually gave up on God. The youth was appearing with friends in my bedroom just before dawn on a regular basis, waking me with abuse and insults, mocking my belief and denigrating my self-worth. I cannot clearly remember the details of what occurred at that time, but the brief moments of memory I retain still send shivers down my spine. This was spiritual intimidation at its worst.

I will not spend too much time in this book describing the works of the enemy as he attempted to destroy me, enough to say that this family member had maintained their connection with the Hamilton-Byrne cult and was attempting to use their repugnant methods to control my mind and capture me in their movement, a process that I resisted throughout. It was the desperation of hopelessness that led me to renew my cry to God, to make a stand and defy the enemy in my house as I struggled to overcome all that had been brought against me.

I found the family member I was caring for administering some sort of drug to my coffee. I then realized why the previous months had been such a blur, why I had lost perspective and become so disoriented. I recalled the practices of the cult he had been involved with and it all began to make sense. They had been drugging my food and drink and were attempting to control my mind as I slept in a drug affected state. I am not sure exactly what substance was administered to me, but I do vaguely recall mention of a drug known as MDA, which I later discovered was a very powerful psychotropic drug, causing massive release of serotonin in the brain, increased heart rate and hallucinations. This was consistent with my experience during that time. At one stage I did not sleep for four days and nights and timed my heart at 180 beats per minute while at rest. My mental processes were completely scrambled for weeks to come.

Shortly after this event in my desperation I attempted to take my life with pills. I can still remember having a sense of the same warm love as I experienced during my death experience as I drifted on the edge of consciousness. I was continuing to take pills with the intention of ending my life when I heard a loud voice say "enough!" and I dropped the pills onto the ground. I do not remember anything from that time but waking up in hospital after having my stomach pumped and simply standing up and walking out of the hospital. I made my way home and continued to battle with my state of mind and the situation I had become entangled in. I am without doubt that it was the insidious tactics of the Hamilton-Byrne cult that had led to my distressed state and near death.

I clearly remember one night in my bed, in the early hours of the morning, surrounded by four of the friends of the family member I had taken into my house, being intimidated and abused by them, having my God insulted by them, when the Spirit of God came upon me mightily. I heard a great voice of authority emerging from deep within me calling out to them loudly, "You cannot have this vessel. Only fools mess with God." In that moment something spiritual broke apart as God's spirit entered into me and they literally ran from the house in fear. At this point I came to God on my knees and begged for His help and praised him for rescuing me from this life-threatening situation. I told that member of my family to leave the house and started praying intensely and regularly, immersing myself in God's presence as much as I could.

From that time onward I could feel God's power returning to me. The battle was not over, but the first round had been won. I sought out a local church and began to attend regularly, joining the worship team and praising God with my musical gifts. My life gradually began to turn around and God restored me and began to bless me. I returned to University to enroll in an honors year and later the Head of School invited me to apply for a PhD scholarship, which I was accepted into and completed the doctorate in the year 2000. My youngest son James was born in 1999 and he has been a great blessing to me. My two daughters, Hannah and Evelyn, continued to grow into beautiful young girls. God was restoring to me what had been lost in those dark years.

A question that has occurred to me on more than one occasion is this: Did the hardship and spiritual attack that came against me have anything to do with God's choice to bring me back to life, to send me back into this world with a message to share? Was there an ongoing battle taking place over my life with the enemy trying to prevent me from reaching the point where my testimony of the death experience could reach people and change lives? Was this an attempted sabotage on God's plan to use me to expand his Kingdom? I cannot help but think that whenever the enemy tries to prevent something from occurring, he inadvertently provides the means by which God enables the very thing the enemy is trying to prevent. He tried to kill Jesus to stop him. As a result, the sins of all humanity were washed away and Jesus became the eternal King, seated at the right hand of God. Not that I would ever compare myself to my Lord, but I do observe a similar pattern. The Devil tried to destroy me and as a result I have now written a book that will (if God wills) spread the good news of the kingdom of heaven, to build hope in a hopeless world, that death is not the end of life, that there is a loving God awaiting all those who call out to him for help.

I have learned much about the way God works through the dimension of time, speaking through his Spirit into the lives of his people, working through the unseen spiritual forces that control our lives, even though we are at most times unaware of their presence around and within us. I believe God saved me from death on more than one occasion in order to spread a message of eternal life. I believe you are now reading the results of the enemy's failed attempt to silence God's voice at work in my life. I believe that if you only surrender to the love of God that permeates the whole universe that you too will experience that incredible love when you leave this mortal body behind.

"For as the heavens are higher than the earth, so are my ways higher than your ways and my thoughts than your thoughts. For as the rain comes down and the snow from heaven and do not return there, but water the earth and make it bring forth and bud, that it may give seed to the sower and bread to the eater, so shall My word be that goes forth from My mouth; it shall not return to Me void, but it shall accomplish what I please and it shall prosper in the thing for which I sent it." [Isaiah 55 9-11 ESV]

God is not easily prevented from achieving his will.

# PART THREE
## UNDERSTANDING

# Introduction to Part Three

The years following my heart attack and death experience have led me to ask many questions and to consider the universal human condition in the light of the things I have been exposed to both physically and spiritually. Part three is an account of the changes that have taken place within me and the growing understanding of the way we function as mortal beings housing an immortal soul. It is an attempt to put profound spiritual experiences into words, so I ask your forgiveness in advance if it does not do the subject matter justice.

Since my return to life I have felt a burning need to rediscover the truth and power of the Lord's heavenly presence while here on earth. The whispering voice of God continues to prompt me to pursue his kingdom. I have a deep belief that Jesus walked this earth with the kingdom of heaven pulsating within him to an extent we cannot even imagine and taught the method of the indwelling of that presence to his disciples. He assures us that the promise of his presence and the indwelling of the Holy Spirit is his will for all believers [John 17:20-21].

Being in his presence has left me with a thirst for that infinite greatness that will not abate with the years. Having tasted of his love I cannot help but strive to revisit the perfection of his being. There is nothing in this life that approaches the richness of the unity of souls when the Lord truly becomes one with his people. The remaining chapters of this book tell of the revelations

I have been given concerning the state of the human heart, the importance of being willing to change, to accept the growth that he wishes for us, even if it does not take the form we may expect.

I do not think the people of Israel in the time of Christ expected a crucified messiah, but what a different world it may have been if they had been open to God in a way they did not expect or control. It is a grave mistake for humanity in our institutions and traditions to start limiting God by squashing him into the mold of our expectations. He will always exceed them. I ask that you read with an open heart, that you remain open to believing that God is readily available to us in ways that we have never considered, simply because we have difficulty believing in something so easy and simple yet so divine.

The condition of our hearts is paramount in our search for God and our ongoing relationship with him. Hardened hearts do not change. Softened hearts allow God to shape them and create a new and fresh condition in the lives of his people. I hope that you can soften your hearts to his word and experience the fullness of his presence in your life, even as I have. The heart is deep within us, at the very core of our being and it is the very site of his authorship in humanity. Be flexible, be willing to be written by him and he promises to lead you into his kingdom to worship at his feet. I stand as a witness to his great desire to come within every person and set them free from the chains that bind people in sadness and separation from his love. As you read the words that follow I ask you to open your hearts to possibility, to the realization that God loves you enough to give a free gift of his life and his presence in your life.

> "He has sent me to bind up the broken hearted, to proclaim freedom for the captives and release from darkness for the prisoners." [Isaiah 61:1 NIV]

# Chapter 8

## The Kingdom of Heaven
## is Within You

By now you have most likely come to the realization that mine has been far from an average life. There have been extremities of pain and suffering and in contrast, moments of exhilaration, of enlightenment and breakthrough. I make no claim to have all the answers to life, having been beyond the doors of death, or to perfectly know God's will. I am a man just like any other, dwelling within a mortal body, subject to the same laws of life and death, good and evil, right and wrong. The great gift that God has granted me is to have had a brief glimpse of eternity and to have taken a short breath of its immeasurable greatness, so see through the curtain of illusion that would have us believe that this life and this world are all that exists and all that matters. To see the face of Jesus and to feel the love that emanates from his glorious being are experiences that will never leave me and I hope and pray that is some small way I have been able to communicate the profound power and significance of that encounter.

It is now several years since I was restored to life. I have recovered well physically, I have gone through a time of adjustment and re-evaluation and have arrived at a place where I now understand that God's will for us in this lifetime is to encounter his eternal kingdom while a we are alive in the flesh. The kingdom of heaven is the subject of many of Jesus' parables, being likened to a pearl of great value, a lost coin that is rediscovered, a small seed that grows into a great tree, a pinch of leaven that leavens a whole loaf of bread and many other illustrative metaphors that Jesus used to explain the role and characteristics of God's kingdom.

From my experience the kingdom of heaven is something more valuable than any other aspect of life. Once encountered it becomes the most importing thing, to discover heaven more completely, to be firmly in possession of that pearl, coin or seed. Once the power, joy and beauty of the kingdom of heaven have been encountered all other aspects of life fade into insignificance. Such a re-ordering of priorities has been my experience. Now that I have seen and tasted the heavenly realm there is nothing in this world that can compare.

After recovering from the heart attack I have been consistently drawn back again to experience the heavenly feeling, the presence and glory of God in my life. The good news is that he has not left me, that I am not imprisoned in a body of flesh that is isolated from the kingdom of heaven.

There is a window to Heaven, through which we can to some extent see, feel and sense the heavenly realm. The wonder of the kingdom of heaven is that once it is within you it grows, it spreads, it affects your whole being, it bears fruit and reproduces, multiplying and bursting through all restraints. That is the leaven or yeast quality of the kingdom. If I do not speak of my direct experience of God's kingdom it threatens to leap out of my mouth without my intention or control. The kingdom of heaven will not be stopped or contained but will continue to infiltrate and change this world until it is eventually victorious and we will all be changed.

If you are in any doubt as to the significance of the kingdom of heaven, just remember the words of Jesus, "I tell you the truth, of all who have ever lived, none is greater than John the Baptist. Yet even the least person in the kingdom of heaven is greater than he is!" [Matt. 11:11 NLT]

The kingdom of heaven surrounds you in every moment of your life and is with you everywhere you go. It is silently present at every moment of decision in your life, waiting to break through the veil that separates the worlds and change the earth forever. It continues to burst out as a spring of living water, to bring life to a dying planet and cause growth in the barren desert of human existence.

The goal of my life and the meaning of my existence have become to seek out and understand "the knowledge of the secrets of the Kingdom of Heaven." [Matt.13:11 NIV.] This simple statement from Jesus contains some important points:

1. The Kingdom of Heaven can be known – hence the "knowledge of the secrets of the Kingdom of Heaven."
2. The knowledge of the Kingdom of Heaven is concealed or secret.
3. Jesus says "it is given to you to know the secrets …" In other words, the secrets of the kingdom of heaven are not known through normal human experience but are a gift from God.

Jesus goes on in this passage to quote the Prophet Isaiah:

> "Though seeing they do not see, though hearing they do not hear or understand." [Matt. 13:13 NIV.]

Clearly Jesus is pointing to a level of spiritual perception that is not readily available to all humanity but is gifted by God. The perception of the kingdom of heaven is not possible without an open heart. As the Prophet Isaiah said: "Make the heart of this people calloused … otherwise they might see with their eyes, hear with their ears, understand with their hearts and turn and be healed". [Isaiah 6:10 NIV]

The Apostle Paul also says: "I pray that the eyes of your heart may be enlightened … that you may know the hope to which he has called you." [Eph 1:18 NIV]

The heart is identified in both these scriptures as a requirement for knowing the kingdom of heaven here and now. An open heart enables the emotional and spiritual state required to recognize and receive the kingdom of heaven. In any search for heaven having a heart that is open and flexible is essential as it allows God to work on the heart, to change it, to shape it and to establish the pathways of communication (seeing, hearing, understanding) that are needed for us to enter into his kingdom.

The seeing, hearing and understanding that we need to develop within ourselves are not of the normal earthly kind. Jesus is directing us toward an inner vision, hearing words directly from God and the understanding of the underlying laws and principles of a purely spiritual kingdom. When I use the word "spiritual" in this context I do not mean that the laws and principles are concerned only with spiritual matters as we know them in the world and refer to the spiritual realm from an earthly perspective, (from the earthly side of the veil,) but that we need to develop eyes, ears and understanding that comprehend and interact with the spiritual forces of the kingdom on the other, heavenly side of the veil. In other words, Jesus is asking us to break through the veil into the kingdom of heaven itself, while living here in the earthly realm. He is asking us to develop (or to allow him to develop within us,) the ability to see visions in the heavenly, to hear words of prophecy, words of knowledge and wisdom in the heavenly and to understand the hidden existence of the heavenly kingdom while walking the path of an earthly life.

How can we as earthly beings even begin to see, hear and understand from the heavenly perspective? Jesus has provided us with some clear guidelines by quoting the prophet [Isaiah 6:9-10 NIV].

He said, "Go and tell this people: 'Be ever hearing, but never understanding; be ever seeing, but never perceiving.' Make the heart of this people calloused; make their ears dull and close their eyes. Otherwise they might see with their eyes, hear with their ears, understand with their hearts, and turn and be healed."

Note the order in which the words are delivered. First comes the order of shutting down the spiritual awareness of the people. The heart becomes calloused, then the ears are made dull, (spiritually) and the eyes are closed (spiritually,) which makes the people unable to understand and know the message of the kingdom. Notice also that the 'opening up' phase occurs in the opposite order. First the spiritual eyes are opened, then the spiritual ears are opened and finally to understand with their hearts and turn and be healed. The spiritual eyes concern visions and dreams, the spiritual ears concern words of divine prophecy, wisdom and understanding. To understand with the heart and turn and be healed involves the acceptance and integration of the kingdom of heaven into the earthly life.

To understand with the heart seems to the contemporary Western mind to be a contradiction. We have been trained to think of the heart and mind as mutually exclusive parts of our being. The mind for knowledge and understanding, the heart for emotions such as love, joy, sadness or fear. I have heard it said that the heart in the bible refers to the innermost thought processes of the mind and yet Jesus clearly delineates between the heart and mind [Luke 10:27 and Mark 12:30] where he identifies the heart, mind, strength (body) and soul as the elements used by the individual to love God. To understand with your heart is to combine heart and mind. The heart works in the realm of emotion, sometimes referred to as "affect," in the sense of having affection and it involves engagement with strong emotional forces.

When the heart combines with the mind, a process we can describe as "understanding with your heart," or to "open the eyes of your heart" a very powerful thing occurs. Belief becomes something that we feel. It is a truth that we both know and love. In everyday terms this means to really GET IT! When we really get the message of God, the presence of the kingdom of heaven in this world within our lives, we cannot help but be transformed and "turn and be healed."

One of the major shortfalls of the Church in the current era has been exactly this; that the word of God has been dealt with intellectually in the age of "reason," isolated from the heart, from emotion, from affect. Why has this occurred? Because a group of philosophers and scientists who did not believe in God concluded that emotions were inferior to intellect, that the five physical senses were all that we could use to measure the entire universe and that unless we could see it with our earthly eyes and hear it with our physical ears that it could not exist.

This has very effectively closed the spiritual eyes and ears of several generations and this short-sighted lie was woven into the fabric of our education, taught as the great truth of our age and was claimed to be a great enlightenment. In reality, this was more of a darkening, as it shut down the spiritual perception of several generations, replacing it with a bland physicality that limited the whole universe to those elements that could be measured only by physical means.

Heaven is not physical. It cannot be measured with scientific instruments, experimented on or researched scientifically. Despite the calling of God in our hearts to believe, the great majority of the Western world followed on blindly, looking to science and reason to provide answers that they were never able to provide. Our hearts were shut down, became hard and calloused. The aspects of the heart were denigrated and denied and the intellect, devoid of emotional attachment, was lauded as the height of human existence.

God is now calling us to come back to the light, to break off the hardened callous from our hearts, to embrace emotional involvement with our understanding, to combine intellectual knowledge with emotional attachment.

To reduce the message of God to a ritual only, or an intellectual exercise is in fact a form of punishment from God. To engage in Christianity as a dry ritual based on rules and regulations, as a series of "do's" and "don'ts," is a contradiction of the intended message of Christ. The prophet Isaiah describes the practice of God's word in the form of ritual without heart attachment as a reason for spiritual downfall:

> "But the word of the Lord was to them, 'Precept upon precept, precept upon precept, line upon line, line upon line, Here a little, there a little,' That they might go and

fall backward and be broken and snared and caught."
[Isaiah 28:13 ESV]

If we practice our belief as a system of intellectual precepts we have completely missed the point of the message and it will soon become dry and devoid of life and relevance. The Christian Church, as with pre-Christian Israel, has gone through its own phase of legalism, precept upon precept, line upon line, do and do, in other words, a long list of intellectual concepts, instructions for living life and laws. Intellectual religion removed from heart attachment and affection becomes a practice of precepts and doctrines and is very similar to the practices of the Pharisees in the time of Jesus. In fact, this approach to the word of God was the leaven of the Pharisees and Sadducees that Jesus warned his disciples against. [Matt. 16: 5-12]

The doctrines and legalistic principles that were being taught by these groups involved a purely legal understanding of the Law of Moses and had become a stale, ritualized religion that resulted from a calloused, ineffective heart, hardened and unchanging, more concerned with rules and instructions than with the love of God. Such a form of intellectually dominated religion locks its followers into a way of being that is unresponsive to hearing the living voice of God. In this time God is calling us to remove the callous from the hearts of all who will hear the message understand it with their hearts and "turn and be healed."

How did God say he would attempt to remove the callous from the hearts of his people?

For with stammering lips and another tongue He will speak to this people, to whom He said, "This is the rest with which You may cause the weary to rest," And, "This is the refreshing." [Isaiah 28:11-12 KJV]

Can this prophecy be referring to any other than Spirit filled Christians? Speaking in tongues is the visible evidence of the indwelling Holy Spirit and bringing rest to the weary and a refreshing are hallmarks of the teachings of Jesus. If you have been baptized in the Holy Spirit and have opened your heart to

God, you have begun the process of "understanding with your heart." Many have also experienced the spiritual gift of prophecy or have seen spiritual visions and dreams. This is evidence of the opening of your spiritual "eyes" and "ears." There is a process and an order in which these things tend to occur, and this is reflected in the words of the prophet quoted by Jesus as cited earlier in this chapter. They describe a closing down process in which the spiritual insight is shut down and an "awakening" process in which the spiritual being is activated.

"Make the heart of this people calloused; make their ears dull and close their eyes. Otherwise they might see with their eyes, hear with their ears, understand with their hearts, and turn and be healed." [Isaiah 6:9-10 NIV].

The shut-down process Isaiah describes in which people become distanced from God:

Step 1: Callous heart – The heart becomes hardened, unresponsive and inflexible, unmerciful, non-forgiving, unloving and set in its ways.

Step 2: Closed ears – People no longer hear the word of God, they cannot comprehend the meaning of God's communication to them, although they may hear the word physically, their inner understanding is absent.

Step 3: Closed eyes – People who have had vision, imaginations of a great future, dreams, both literal and figurative and even direct visualizations of God, no longer see the hope of the future, or the images that would lead them closer to God's presence and his will for their lives.

This process works on many levels. Once the heart is hardened, the spiritual hearing of a people is diminished, and a form of spiritual deafness ensues. Mercy, love and compassion are overlooked and the voice of God into the heart of his people is progressively ignored. The result of this is that the vision of the people is affected. This brings to mind the proverb: "When there is no prophetic vision the people cast off restraint, but the one who keeps the law, blessed is he!" [Prov. 29:18 NET]

A purely written code, to the exclusion of direct spiritual input from God, loses its power in the spiritual dimension and is limited to the realm of intellect. It becomes a theoretical rather than a practical belief. In the absence of vision, guidance and direction from God the people become directionless and wander aimlessly. When law is combined with vision, the people have restraint, direction and a clear destination. The shutting down process described above is the state in which many traditional churches find themselves in and certainly the state in which the secular world exists. Physical life can continue in the absence of spiritual vision and hearing, but the spirit will wither in the absence of God's direct input.

"Otherwise they might see with their eyes, hear with their ears, understand with their hearts, and turn and be healed." [Isaiah 6:9-10 NIV].

The reverse process described by the prophet is a reversal of the shutdown process. If we expect that Jesus is now calling us to the "awakening" process, the opening of the human soul to God's direct spiritual influence, then we will go through the following stages:

Step 1: Open eyes – We will have a sense of the future, of a purpose that God is working towards in our life. We may well experience dreams that communicate to us directly God's will and purpose for us. We may literally see visions, of Jesus, of Heavenly light, of the future, of non-intellectual spiritual concerns that guide us or spiritually nurture us. Such phrases as "seeing possibilities" or getting a "glimpse of the future" will be the simple everyday manifestation of this process, whereas literal visions of future events or of goals and destinations for your life are the more complete and spiritually driven manifestation of the opening of the inner eyes.

Step 2: Open ears – We begin to hear the voice of God speaking directly to our spirit, through the words of others, the words of the scriptures, or even coincidental combinations of events and words in the media that combine to tell us what is God's will for our lives. Once again this is the simplest everyday manifestation of open ears, the more complete spiritual manifestation is to hear God's still small voice within your inner self and distinguish his communication from your own internal dialog. This eventually grows into words of prophecy, words of wisdom or words of knowledge. These are the literal "charisms" or gifts of the Holy Spirit as described in Paul's letter to the Romans [Rom. chapters 12–14]. Many who have experienced the gift of tongues will recognize that this plays a big part in opening one's ears to hear God's voice in the inner person.

Step 3: Understanding with the heart - To accept that some of the voice activity we comprehend within our mind is not purely psychological in its origin, but it is God's presence deep within our soul talking to us, is a huge step in coming to know God. We do well to listen and heed the inner voices that continually debate and discuss, respond to life and offer advice to ourselves deep within the inner person. In time we learn to recognize the still, small voice of God in among the chatter of the mind and come to rely on its presence. Learning to recognize the presence of God in our dreams, in our "imaginations" and in direct spiritual visions, develops through the hearing of God's voice in our souls, into the understanding of God in our hearts. Seeing God, hearing his voice and finally responding to him in a heart-felt, emotional and passionate way, is the third and most powerful stage of the awakening or "opening up" process. The end result is to "turn and be healed." It is the response to God's prompting that fulfills the healing and awakening that God desires in your life.

One extremely memorable aspect of my death experience was the way I could see in the spiritual realm although I was not using physical eyes. This was an experience I had encountered before in dreams that seemed extremely vivid and in a few Holy Spirit inspired visions. We can see with our soul. I saw angels. I saw the Lord. I saw images of my own future life, however brief and fleeting. I am convinced now more than ever that there is a form of spiritual vision that is just as significant as spiritual hearing. Jesus was of course fully conversant with this ability.

Jesus was able to see Nathaniel under the fig tree before Philip came to call him. [John 1:48] There are times, even now many years after the event, when I can dimly see the face of Jesus in my "mind's eye," or, as I now prefer to call it, with spiritual vision. Having been in his presence in the spirit it is easier for me now to discern his spiritual presence in my physical life and to realize that he was equally present prior to the death experience. All that has changed since that time is my ability to recognize his presence as the result of having been with him in the absence of my physical body and being familiar with that sensation. It is my belief that Jesus is present and near to us far more than most people are aware of and that he works within us often without our being aware of his presence.

Many Christians believe that historically this is a time of increased Holy Spirit activity and that dreams and visions are a significant part of that awakening, as spoken by the prophet Joel:

> "And afterward, I will pour out my Spirit on all people.
> Your sons and daughters will prophesy, your old men
> will dream dreams, your young men will see visions.
> [Joel 2:28 NIV]

The apostle Peter also quotes this passage in Acts 2:17-21, as he announces the onset of the age of the Holy Spirit on the day of Pentecost in Jerusalem. Note that this prophecy identifies three forms of evidence that the Holy Spirit is poured out on the people, firstly prophecy, then dreams and finally visions. These signs are used to indicate that the Holy Spirit is being poured out on the people.

What then is our role in this outpouring of God's Spirit and is it happening to us in this present time? There is a tendency in all things concerned with the gifts of the Holy Spirit to assume that we are passive receivers of the gifts, that they simply "happen to us." Many assume that we have no control over the presence or absence of the gifts of the Holy Spirit. On the contrary, we have a responsibility to exercise and encourage the gifts of God in our lives.

> "Do not neglect your gift, which was given you through prophecy when the body of elders laid their hands on you." [I Tim. 4:14 NIV]

> "Fan into flame the gift of God which is within you through the laying on of my hands." [2 Tim. 1:6 NIV]

> "The spirits of prophets are subject to the control of prophets." [I Cor. 14:32 NIV]

Not only are the gifts subject to our control, but we can influence which of the gifts we receive:

> "For this reason the one who speaks in a tongue should pray that they may interpret what they say." [I Cor. 14:13 NIV]

We *can control* the gifts of the spirit and can request that gifts be activated. The same is true of our spiritual vision. In Old Testament times there was a school of the prophets in which men were trained in the knowledge of the spiritual gifts and how to pass on, share and mentor others in those gifts. (See I Sam. 19:20, II Kings 2:15, II Kings 4:1, II Kings 4:38. II Kings 6:1-7). The school of the prophets took an active role in training up prophets; the gifts that were evident in their activities were prophecy, healing, working miracles and supernatural provision. It is clear that in New Testament times the gifts of the Holy Spirit could be controlled, requested, taught and passed on through the laying on of hands.

I believe there is a call from God to resume the training, teaching and mentoring of believers in the use of the spiritual gifts. We need a greater emphasis on understanding with the heart and rediscovering the power of the Holy Spirit to turn lives around, heal us of the calloused hearts that many of us may not have been aware we had. I believe there is a call from God for Christians to feel as well as think, to see in the spirit as well as hearing and to understand with our hearts. Open the eyes of our hearts Lord! What would this process look like? Firstly, it would involve us getting to know ourselves in all the aspects of our being, as heart, mind, body and soul.

This would mean us spending some time and effort learning to distinguish between the mental processes that are given precedence in contemporary Western society and the working of our emotions, not as an unwelcome intrusion on our thoughts, but as an essential companion to the mind. This requires more than merely recognizing that there is a place for emotion, that it has validity and a right to exist within our being, but also giving it the recognition it requires as a significant and essential part of our being.

The biblical usage of the word for heart implies a union of inner thoughts and emotions. The heart in the Bible refers to the core of a person's being:

1. Where their intentions are formed and actions are planned. Mark 12:33. Gen. 6:5, Ex. 9:14, Ps. 64:9, 105:25, 140:2.
2. Where tenderness, softness or hardness are formed. II Kings 22, Job 23:16.
3. Purity and cleanliness are observed, Ps 24:4, 51:10
4. Wisdom and understanding are reached. Job 38:36, Prov. 2:2,
5. Faith is practiced. Mark 11:23
6. It is most certainly the central point of relationship with God and requires change and growth for us to enter into

a full union with him: Ps. 86:11, 119:10, 34, 58, 69, 145, Prov4:23, Ezek 36:26, Rom10:8-10, Eph. 3:16-17.

7. The heart is clearly contrasted to the activities of the mind: Phil. 4:7, Isaiah 29:13.

The heart is the inner person, the hidden personal place where our ideas form and our attitudes, plans and intentions are given shape. Our emotions clearly play a significant part in the process, both as a driving force that *forms* our ideas and in the resulting states of being that are the *consequences of* the condition of our heart. The heart is the innermost secret place that defines who I am. Although the heart may be responsible for forming our actions it is distinct from the outer expression of our lives. It is the part of us where our secret desires, fear, hopes lusts, joy, anger, love, courage and mercy all take shape. It is a melting pot of thoughts, feelings and emotions in which we form our responses that are then transformed by the mind into our actions. God tries and tests our hearts. God lifts up our hearts. More than that, Jesus lives within our hearts. [Eph. 3:16-17].

When I was with the Lord my strongest memory and the greatest experience I had was that my heart was glowing, throbbing and full to bursting point with love, joy and peace. I could not contain the richness of the love he put into my heart. That was the pure and complete experience of the kingdom of heaven. I have rediscovered that experience here in the earthly realm on several occasions, albeit in a reduced form, but this has taught me that the kingdom of heaven can be invoked from our physical state, pass through the invisible veil between earth and heaven and set our hearts alight here and now. It is the expression of the presence of Jesus in the earth.

A portal between heaven and earth exists within our hearts. The way for Jesus to enter into the world and work in the physical domain is within you. The way to open up this portal is faith, believing in your heart and inviting Jesus to come in and inhabit your being. The extent to which he will enter in is directly proportional to the level of your faith, your ability to believe that he is within you.

We limited humans have many doubts to overcome, assumptions that must be dismissed and fears to be pushed aside before Jesus has a clear passage into our hearts. If you believe in your heart that the Son of God stands at the door and knocks and if you truly take the step of opening the door wide, you have his promise that he will enter.

Some people have many bars and locks on their doorways. Fear keeps them huddled within, afraid of letting anything enter in. For God's love to truly flood into a person's being they must remove the locks and bars. Fears must be overcome, doubts dismissed, hatred forgotten and offences forgiven, lust and pride must be abandoned. One word can summarize this process. Surrender! As you read these words, identify the resistance you feel within and simply surrender it to him. Open the door and invite him in with no restraints, no doubts and no fears. Let his light and love flood into the dark chamber within. Be aware of the visualization that you use as you envisage him entering in and filling your being with light. Notice the warmth in your heart as you accept the reality of his presence. Be content that he has made his home within you and know that the kingdom of heaven has come into you today.

# Chapter 9

## Love like a River

The notion of bringing the kingdom of heaven to earth is hardly a new one. It was at the center of Jesus' mission on Earth and was never far from his mind as he taught, healed, admonished and encouraged the people of Israel. He described the kingdom of heaven as being variable, being either near or far, accessible (with the keys to the kingdom) and, most importantly, habitable by people here on earth. Jesus statement "the least in the kingdom of heaven is greater than he," was referring to living believers on earth.

The purpose of this book is to communicate the very idea that heaven is accessible and inhabitable by us as we walk the earth, not only after death, but now as we live and breathe. Christians who are familiar with the terminology of the New Testament will most likely respond by saying that all those who believe that Jesus is the Son of God are in the kingdom of heaven. I do not think it is quite so clear cut. If that was the case, how could the kingdom of heaven be "near" or "far" when Jesus himself was present? The factor that indicated the presence of the kingdom was the supernatural alteration of events on earth by heavenly forces. This sometimes took the form of repentance and changes in people's lives, at other times healing and supernatural spiritual gifts. Actions that change the earth, people on earth, physical states or conditions through the agency of God's power are the indication of the presence of the kingdom of heaven on earth during Jesus ministry.

"Repent for the kingdom of heaven has come near." [Matt. 4:17 NIV]

"And the power of the Lord was with Jesus to heal the sick." [Luke 5:17 NIV] (By implication there were some times when the power was not with him to do so, as unbelief prevented the working of the kingdom.)

"And he sent them out to proclaim the kingdom of God and to heal the sick." [Luke 9:2 NIV]

"My kingdom is not of this world." [John 18:36 NIV]

Some Christians today tend to set the boundaries of the kingdom of heaven very firmly around the churches that they attend. I believe we are missing out on a great deal by assuming that the kingdom as referred to by Jesus is merely a synonym for the church. The kingdom of heaven is an entirely different system of authorities and powers at work and that system is in stark contrast with the authorities and systems that operate in this world. Time holds no sway; disease has no place in God's kingdom and is repelled from its presence. Worldly wealth is of little use in God's kingdom, only as a means of exchanging it for those qualities that are of heavenly value, by using it to express love, hope and faith by giving to those in need, by contributing to agencies of God's kingdom and working on earth to achieve heavenly goals.

Miracles are a sure sign of the presence of the kingdom, as the earthly order is displaced and replaced by the heavenly order of priorities. When the kingdom is present, sadness retreats only to be replaced by joy. Sickness retreats to be replaced by health. Despair retreats to be replaced by hope and hatred is overcome by love. Both the inner being and the physical body are transformed and made better by the mere presence of the kingdom of heaven.

This power is unquestionably at work in many churches today, but to think of the church as equivalent to God's kingdom is to miss the point altogether. As we have discussed earlier, the kingdom of heaven is a state of growth, an explosive force that, once experienced, cannot easily be forgotten but will emerge from within and demand our full attention. If you have felt within you a love that is unexplainable in human terms, that warms your heart and fills your mind with its goodness generosity and flows into your actions, then you have experienced to some extent the kingdom of heaven. Where love overflows in the heart of a person and overflows into the lives of others around them, the kingdom of heaven is at work. The passing on of gifts, wisdom, understanding, knowledge and truth are also kingdom transactions. These things all bring about a change in the earthly existence and bring it into closer alignment with the will of heaven.

There is however a question of measure. I have felt in the presence of Jesus a power so strong and gentle, all-consuming yet non-intrusive, completely supernatural and yet so familiar it felt more like home than being held in my mother's arms. The power of his kingdom can and does flow through us and into this world. The challenge for us is to allow this flow to occur to its maximum capacity without standing in the way and inhibiting its effectiveness. Jesus plainly told us that the essential elements for acting in the kingdom are love and faith. If we can learn to believe *completely* in his presence within us and in his ability to change the course of events in this world, then the flow will occur, and heaven will pass through us and into this world. Belief is the key to enabling the flow of heaven's power and love is the key to directing the flow.

This is more than another sermon on being kind to those around you, although that is of course admirable and an essential part of the Christian life. This is a call to understand that the utilization of love and faith as a means of bringing the kingdom of heaven to earth takes our inner spiritual state into a new and more powerful dimension.

Love and faith in action enable the windows of heaven to be opened, the outpouring of God's power into this world and bringing about direct changes in earthly life. Faith, a pure belief in the power of God to achieve all things, is the normal situation in the heavenly realm. There is no doubt in heaven about God's ability to work miracles, to heal the sick, to be present in all places and times, or even his ability to raise the dead. There is no sickness or death in heaven. Heaven operates in that state continuously and looking back on the earthly existence from that perspective did make me marvel at the blindness that reigns over humanity. Belief should be our natural state as citizens of heaven. It is doubt that inhibits the flow of heaven's will and power into the earth.

Two examples of Jesus' ministry come immediately to mind. When a man came to Jesus complaining that the disciples could not cast the demon out of his son, Jesus response was firstly to cast the demon out himself and then to explain that it was unbelief that had prevented the disciples from being able to cure the boy. He then went on to teach that belief and faith make anything possible, even moving a mountain. [Matt. 17:14-21] The emphasis Jesus put on this event was not, (to paraphrase,) 'It's alright, you tried your best, but you didn't have enough faith to work this mighty miracle. That's OK because this was a tough one.' On the contrary, he said it was because of their unbelief that the miracle did not occur, as if they had prevented what was, to Jesus, a normal course of events. Several times Jesus rebuked his disciple for their unbelief which prevented miracles from occurring. Let us truly come to understand this concept, because within this understanding lies the key to grasping the power of the kingdom of heaven.

If we do not absolutely believe that a miracle will occur, then we are out of alignment with the kingdom of heaven. We must stop seeing faith as something that must be painstakingly built up and come to understand it as a normal condition. Miracles will happen. God will intervene. It is our unbelief and our "anti-faith" that will stop the flow of heaven into earth.

"I do believe, but help me overcome my unbelief!" [Mark 9:24 NLT] It is also important to remember that Jesus could not do many miracles in his hometown because the people there did not believe. [Matt.13:58] Unbelief is a miracle stopper. Unbelief closes the window to heaven.

It is immensely valuable to consider the greatest weapon of heaven, which is love.

"God is love." [I John 4:8 NLT]

"Three things will last forever - faith, hope, and love - and the greatest of these is love." [I Cor. 13:13 NLT]

Once we have opened the window of heaven with our faith, the flow of God's power and love is free to enter the kingdom of earth. But what is the nature of this mysterious power that transforms lives, restores broken hearts and reduces hard-hearted humanity to tears with such ease? I have seen many people when confronted with the presence of God's Spirit weep uncontrollably for no apparent reason. Many of them later describe this experience as a release of pent up emotion that has been locked up inside and is suddenly freed to flow as the power of heaven streams into their hearts.

Such was my experience in the presence of the Lord. All barriers were removed, and he was able to move freely into parts of me I had always considered my private inner world, my own inner sanctum. I could literally feel his presence inside my soul, becoming a part of my thoughts and feelings, engaging with the very core of what I call 'myself.' His presence within me was enlivening, liberating and all powerful, sweeping aside all fears, resistance and reservations, but with such gentle power I was glad for the intrusion. As he entered into my soul I was able to sense his being and experience his presence in such a complete way that I was both overwhelmed and exhilarated by the dimensions of his awareness and the irresistible power of his love. I knew as I had never known before the complete meaning of the words "God IS love."

Being filled with his love in the spiritual realm has given me a vastly altered understanding of God as love, God being made up of love, consisting of love. His manifestation on the earth is in the love we show to other people, not just our friends and family. It is in the love we display towards people we are not expected to love. When we love someone above and beyond expectations we break the chains that hold the people of this world captive. We create a flow from heaven through us into others and often this creates a flow of love that in turn flows on to another, to another, to another and changes the spiritual atmosphere of this world.

"So now I am giving you a new commandment: Love each other. Just as I have loved you, you should love each other." [John 13:34 NLT]

"I have revealed you to them, and I will continue to do so. Then your love for me will be in them, and I will be in them." [John 17:26 NLT]

God's love is meant to flow like a river, from the Father, through the Son, the Holy Spirit, into us and then on into others. This command is at the core of Jesus mission on earth. If God is love, then *when we love other people we are directly putting God into their lives.* We have heard the command to love one another since we were children. The command is nothing new. The revelation I have been given concerning love is to come to a more complete understanding of what it is we are doing when we love one another and why Jesus would have given this very simple command such a primary position of importance in his ministry.

God is love. Literally! The force we experience in our lives as love is presence of God himself. When we love one another we transfer the presence of God from one person to another, even if we do not name it as such, even if we are unaware that we are spreading the presence of God. Love is the highest form of human action. It is as close as we can come to being God in this earthly existence. When we operate in love, we are operating within the person of God; we are operating as the presence of God.

I have felt the love of God in a way that very few have been privileged to know. This love will change your life if you remove the callouses, unblock the channels by removing resistance and allow it to flow like a river through your life and into others. It is a gentle love that will not force itself on you. It is your challenge to develop the skill of having no resistance, of clearing the channels through which love flows. It is a love that is felt in the heart but is in complete harmony with the intellect. It is a transformational love that alters all that it touches, merely through its presence.

It is precisely because this love is gentle and kind that it is so easily stopped by unbelief. The particular belief that is required is a belief in the reality of God's love within your being, its power to transform and its healing presence. Even as I write and as you read, I sense this love at work in my heart and I hope in yours also. I experience warmth in my inner being and I believe as you read that warmth is present within you also. The words I now write have been inspired by the presence of Jesus.

His presence is promised to all who believe in him [John 17:20-21] I have come to know and recognize his presence intimately since meeting with him in the spirit. That experience taught me how to allow the spirit of God to flow through me relatively unhindered and has helped me to believe unreservedly in his presence and power in my life. It is also not only possible, but easily achieved by any person who believes in Jesus as the Son of God and accepts his presence right here and right now, with the innocence and trust that a child has in a parent.

Practice the presence of God by simply knowing it is true, it is within you now and accepting that it is very, very powerful. Close your eyes and see his face in front of yours. Ask him to make his home within you and remove all the barriers that would keep him out. I have felt his power and presence, I have experienced his universal awareness and I can personally guarantee that if you speak to him in your inner person, he will hear what you say. If you believe in his presence simply and completely, without intellectual restraint or doubt, he will come into you and make his home in your heart and soul. It is good to reinforce your faith with your words. I believe. I believe. I believe.

"For God so loved the world that he gave his one and only Son, that whoever *believes* in him shall not perish but have eternal life." [John 3:16 NIV]

I can give personal assurance that this is true. I died, however briefly, and because I called on him and believed in him, I know that even if he had not sent me back to live in my body, I would have lived forever in his presence. Of this you do have my personal guarantee and assurance. His promises are true and death has no victory over those who believe in him.

# Chapter 10

## Vision

I have written this book to bear witness to the truth, to the God of truth and to his amazing Son who lives in the heavens and possesses power, knowledge and wisdom beyond our wildest dreams. His face is always before my eyes, provided I can put the distractions of this world aside and see him as I once saw him in the spiritual body. It is the constant tugs and persuasions of the cares and distractions of this world that stand in the way of us seeing his face clearly in every moment of our lives. The great realization that I hope you can now share in your own life is that he has always been very close, right before my eyes, even before my heart attack and death experience, looking me in the face and sharing his love with me. I simply did not recognize his presence for what it truly was until I passed out of this physical body to meet him in the spirit. Now his real and tangible presence is a constant in my life whenever I take the time and make the effort to clear away the dross and focus on him.

His presence is so remarkably familiar and gentle, soft and caring, yet as strong as a mighty river. Those who have declared with their voice that he is their Lord are assured that his presence will be in their life from that time onward. The difficulty for we intellectually programmed Westerners is to believe and accept that something so familiar, so simple and easy, but also so supernatural can be readily available to us in this harsh physical existence. Many of us have spent so much of our lives striving to learn, training our minds to be analytical and discerning, that we tend to forget that his yoke is easy and his burden is light. The Father has revealed his love to the simple, sending his Son into the world and there is nothing complex or intellectually challenging about that simple act of love.

We have been offered the free gift of eternal life. All that is required of us is to believe in him and follow his commandment of love. How unfortunate that we feel obliged to complicate the issue with degrees in theology, doctrines and religious traditions, being well-read and highly educated. God values a loving heart above all these things. That is not to say that education is wrong in itself, but it is important that we recognize the danger of it obscuring the fact that his message of love is simple.

I have spent ten years of my life studying at university, another twenty years lecturing, and yet the most sublime experience I have had in my lifetime was simply to surrender to God's love and to bask in his presence when I encountered him in the heavenly realm. This was more like a small child totally contented, lying in its mother's arms than any sense of intellectual achievement. It is nothing I could ever work towards or earn by my actions or intellect. It is a simple act of trust and acceptance and belief that God loves me, his creation and that he sent Jesus to rescue me from death. I thank him forever for that!

One of the things that has limited the development of our spiritual ears and eyes as Western Christians is the way we use and understand prayer. We talk to God. It is not often that we have been taught to stop, listen, look and expect a response from God. When we truly believe in God and expect an answer from him in the same way as we would from a friend or from an earthly father, then we will indeed stop, listen, look, to see and hear his responses. We will learn to expect his conversation, advice, vision and wisdom, evident in our lives as spiritual gifts, insights, foreknowledge and various other supernatural outpourings of the Holy Spirit that occur when we give him the time and space to work within us. To do this we need to be willing to change and develop our prayer techniques.

Prayer and meditation are both a part of the same process of communication with God. Not a descent into emptiness, but a silencing of the mental chatter to enable his voice to be heard among the cacophony. A closing of the eyes not to enter darkness, but to see through the darkness into the spiritual light that lies beyond the veil. This sort of prayer and meditation goes well beyond a list of requests. It is more of a conversation and a communion. Once we believe in the presence of God completely we can no longer be satisfied with a prayer life that consists of only a list of demands: Heal me, provide for me, forgive me, and help me. Like a child who gradually matures and begins to ask its parents for the things that will help it to understand the world more completely, so Christians need to move beyond request based prayer into conversational communion with God and to enter the relatively unexplored area of hearing his spiritual voice and seeing the spiritual visions he gives to us.

Naturally this is not an easy and immediate process, but it requires time and dedication. For some time after my return from death to life I searched for that close communion with Jesus that I had felt in his presence. There were times when I could spontaneously feel his presence and other times when I consciously created the conditions that were needed to enable him to reveal himself. There is a certain feeling, the warm love in my heart, a feeling of a flow of goodness and life emanating from my chest that fills me with a sense of wellbeing. This is the physical indication of his presence; the feeling of being with someone who loves you deeply. The path toward him involves embracing that sensation and allowing it to grow within. This involves the opening of your heart to Jesus as a real and tangible presence within you, as a spiritual reality in the physical world. This is the spiritual awareness of Jesus and his angelic host attending to you here in your earthly life.

Seeking his face, surrender, thankfulness, ascension, worship, anointing and unity mark the path that leads to the full assimilation of God into your life. These are not merely expressions of a state of mind but are a series of stages to pass through on the journey into the heavenly temple and into complete unity with God. I will now share with you what I experienced when I first truly decided to surrender completely and let God take my heart, mind and soul where he would lead them. I had decided that I would dedicate myself to rediscovering his heavenly presence as it was when I was with him, here on earth. I prayed intently to him to show me how to come into his presence in the same way I had experienced in the spirit. I was directly seeking the fullness of his presence while living here in this earthly life.

I spent time in prayer reading the Psalms and other New Testament scriptures that spoke of his greatness. I was then led to sing to him, and to speak out the names of God in Hebrew, as listed below:

- Jahweh = Lord
- Elohim = God
- Shaddai = Almighty
- Jeshua = Jesus
- A Meshiach = The messiah, Christ, anointed one.
- Ruach = Spirit,
- Quaddesh = Holy

I then prayed in my heavenly language (tongues,) until a deep sense of peace came over me. Sitting quietly I simply concentrated on the presence of Jesus within me and totally surrendered to his will. I allowed the physical darkness of having my eyes closed to pass and eventually felt a bright light beginning to form behind the darkness and overwhelm the darkness with light. At this point I surrendered the will of my vision to him, allowing the vista within my mind to be led wherever he would take it. This required a surprising amount of trust and a good deal of self-control, to let go and allow this experience to proceed the way he chose to lead it. I totally gave over my intellect to his control and followed where he led.

The first thing to enter my mind was a line from Psalm100: "Enter his gates with thanksgiving and his courts with praise; give thanks to him and praise his name." [Psalm100:4 NIV]

Other psalms also came to mind:

"Open for me the gates of the righteous; I will enter and give thanks to the Lord." [Psalm 118:19 NIV]

The concept of entering the city of God resonated in my head and I later recalled other references to this idea, such as in Revelation 22:14 "Blessed are those who wash their robes, that they may have the right to the tree of life and may go through the gates into the city." [Revelation 22:14 NIV]

## ENTER

I allowed a vision to form in my mind and saw myself walking along a steep track up to the gates of the city, a stone wall to the right side, a steep rocky slope to the left, as I ascended to the gates and entered in. As I passed through the gates I put my hand on the stones of the wall and thanked God for the city, his heavenly Jerusalem. As I entered the city in the vision I felt a profound change take place within myself, as if I had entered a room full of people and I heard the whispering of many hushed voices.

## SURRENDER

I felt the presence of God strongly in the place and in the people around me, quietly walking through a courtyard and praying with soft voices. I approached one of the people there and asked where I was and who were the people walking about in the streets of the city. He said to me that I was in the city of God, Zion and that these were those who were praying in the spirit on earth. Within that place there were angels and the souls of the faithful in prayer. I was within the heavenly city of god in which the existence of humanity and angels was combined in the act of true spiritual prayer. The angels were mingling with the quietly praying souls, stopping to whisper in their ears, touching them and obviously connected with them spiritually. I gave over all mental control and allowed the deeply reverent state of prayer to wash over me. I remained conscious, but fully immersed in the vision I was experiencing.

## THANKFULNESS

After some time I heard singing and looked toward the upper side of the courtyard and saw a group forming, clapping their hands and singing in a language I did not understand and yet I sensed the meaning of their words. They were singing praise to God. I approached them and they beckoned to me to join them, which I did. The group began to dance and wound their way through the streets of the city, singing and dancing in call and response patterns as they made their way upward away from the gates and into the city. I knew within myself that we were ascending toward the temple.

I felt within me a deep sense of gratitude and thankfulness that I was a part of this group and that I was able to be there in their presence, seeing the city and singing God's praise. The emotions of that moment were expressed in the songs and it was as if the feeling of thankfulness became embodied in the song, the dance and the ascension toward the temple. I felt a love for God deep in my heart and thanked him with every part of my being. The themes of the songs were of his goodness, the love he has for his people, the strength and protection he offers his creation and the power he has placed within us. His love, goodness and mercy were expressed in every movement, note and hand clap as we approached the temple, which I could now see above us.

## ASCEND

As the group approached the temple there was a flight of stone stairs leading up to the temple walls. We ascended the stairs and stood on the edge of the portico at the entrance to the temple court. A silence fell upon us and we were approached by an angelic figure who stood in front of me. He was quite tall and leaned over me as he spoke and said, "Receive the seal of the living God and enter into his temple." He then touched me on the forehead and I felt a surge of power come from his hand flowing into me. With the act of ascending the stairs and being touched I felt a lift in my heart and exhilaration in my mind as I was invited to enter and I knew that I had been somehow raised to a new and higher level of unity with God. As I stepped through the portico and into the inner courtyard I felt the sky above me open, like a cloud had passed and now the sky was clear and open to the heavens.

## WORSHIP

Within there were many people gathered, kneeling and standing with heads bowed in worship of God. There was a profound feeling of awe and reverence. I felt a song rise within me, but not like any normal song. It began with a deep resonating hum from far down within me and began to rise in clear notes through the scale and up to the higher registers of sound. This was my soul singing, not my physical voice. I heard the notes within me and felt them resonating through my body. The notes of the song rose higher until they passed beyond the range of normal human voice and into a pure glassy tone that went even beyond the range of hearing.

It was as if there was a scale of notes ascending through my body, out the top of my head and into the height above, rising ever higher as my soul rejoiced in the presence of God and the open heaven above me. As the song continued to reach higher I felt myself to be connected to a rope that was suspended from above and that appeared to have no end. My song was climbing ever upward and breaking through the sky and into new layers of heaven as my soul rejoiced in the experience and soared to the heights. I began to understand the nature of Jacob's ladder, the angels ascending and descending, the levels of heaven that stretched between our earthly existence and the throne room of God above. I felt a moment of absolute breakthrough where I caught a glimpse of the heavenly throne and was overwhelmed with a surge of power flowing through me and found my thoughts once again within the court of the temple among the faithful gathered there.

## ANOINTING

I heard a voice calling to me across the crowd, asking me to come up to him. I made my way through the crowd and to another flight of stairs that led up to a raised porch. There stood a man dressed in a white robe who beckoned to me to climb the stairs. I ascended and knelt in front of him. He welcomed me and said that he was to anoint me with oil. He found a vessel of oil and tipped it slowly over my head as he said, "I anoint you in the name of the Father". As I was experiencing this vision, I could physically feel a sensation of something running over my hair and down onto my shoulders. I felt almost lightheaded and knew that something had changes within me. He then reached for a second vessel and said, "I anoint you in the name of the Son," and once again poured the oil over my head. This time I felt a glowing warmth in my heart as the oil ran down over me. This was the same sensation I had felt in the presence of Jesus while 'dead' and separated from my body, it was an experience of ultimate love, comfort and joy.

Once again he reached for another vessel and said, "I anoint you in the name of the Holy Spirit," and tipped the contents over me. This time I felt a warm pressure at the base of my throat, a building pressure that felt as if I would explode if I did not give it expression with my voice. The pure joy and exhilaration of this moment was astounding. Although I was sitting still in a chair while seeing this vision, my heart was beating quickly, my whole being was set alight by the sensations that were flowing through my body and mind. He then spoke to me, assuring me that I am loved by God and that he had a purpose for me. He said I was anointed as a king and a priest, which immediately reminded me of I Peter 2:9 "But you are a chosen people, a royal priesthood, a holy nation, God's special possession, that you may declare the praises of him who called you out of darkness into his wonderful light." He told me I should share this moment with many people and that I should bear witness of these things. He then told me to enter the Holy Place, so I stood and walked through another portico entrance into another smaller area.

## UNITY

Within I saw angels seated to the side of the court. One of the angels was singing in a deep, strong and powerful voice, loud enough to shake the floor, deep enough to make me tremble with its resonance. He sang out the name JAH in a prolonged monotone. The power of this sound seemed to echo out from the temple and into the very fabric of the universe, shaking the particles that hold all things together. Although this was fearsomely powerful I was not afraid of these angels. Every now and again another angel would sing in a higher tone like a trumpet blast. Another angel was standing within the court and came to me, telling me not to speak to the singing angels but that I should enter the holy of holies. I started to have my doubts as to my worthiness to enter such a sacred place, but he told me the Lord wanted me to enter. I walked the length of the courtyard and approached the curtain there. I felt the need to take off my shoes, (yes I was wearing shoes in the vision,) so I knelt and removed the shoes from my feet and entered through the curtain and remained on my knees, crawling on all fours. I looked up to see the golden ark at the far end of the room. Above it was a cloud, swirling and flashing with what looked to be electrical currents. I was completely overwhelmed with the power of this vision and remained on my knees until a voice told me to come forward. I crawled toward the cloud and stayed low. Then the voice told me to thrust my head forward into the cloud. At first I did not want to do this as I was afraid of the power contained in the cloud and that it could harm me.

The voice spoke once again, instructing me to put my head into the cloud. I leaned forward and felt the power in the cloud enter my head like two lightning bolts searing into my mind. I remained there for some time, being filled with this power and I literally felt like a battery being charged. I felt strength enter me and I knew the presence of God was strongly within me at that moment. I could not see him, but I felt his greatness all around and within me. Although I doubted my right to be there, into my mind came the words of the book of Hebrews, which says in Chapter 10:19-22: "Therefore, brethren, since we have confidence to enter the holy place by the blood of Jesus, by a new and living way which He inaugurated for us through the veil, that is, His flesh and since we have a great priest over the house of God, let us draw near with a sincere heart in full assurance of faith, having our hearts sprinkled clean from an evil conscience and our bodies washed with pure water." [Hebrews 10:19-22 NIV]

This was the same presence of God I had experienced in death and yet I was fully conscious, alive and firmly within my physical body. This was a spiritual vision that rocked me with its power, its significance and its vivid reality. I now fully realized the significance of the words from the letter to the Hebrews that we can enter the holy place through the body of Jesus. I realized that this is a literal spiritual entry into the temple and into the holy of holies, that Jesus has given us free access into the presence of the Father. The temple of God is truly within us and also in heaven. The two meet within us and we can enter the heavenly temple from within our own being if we allow God to show us the way through his Holy Spirit. God truly does have his dwelling, his house within us. He lives within our heart and soul. Can you believe that something so ultimately divine can be so easily accessible within your own being? That is the heart of the new Covenant that Jesus made with his followers. He wants us to enter a temple that is not an earthly one but is a heavenly temple within us.

"But when Christ came as high priest of the good things that are now already here, he went through the greater and more perfect tabernacle that is not made with human hands, that is to say, is not a part of this creation. He did not enter by means of the blood of goats and calves; but he entered the Most Holy Place once for all by his own blood, thus obtaining eternal redemption." [Hebrews 9:11-12 NIV]

Through this vision and the death experience I have come to believe that we have access to the presence of God and of his Son Jesus far more easily and openly than we have understood in the past. Not only can we have communication with him through prayer, but through spiritual connection we can see visions, hear his voice and meet him in person while in the physical world. Within us we have an open portal to heaven if we can simply believe and accept that the way is open. God's promises to us that he would open the way into the holy of holies through his son Jesus are not vain promises. God always means what he says. We have unfortunately taken it upon ourselves to believe that we have to work to earn the right to come into the heavenly temple and that something so glorious simply must be difficult to achieve and must take a lifetime of self-restraint and harsh discipline to achieve. Usually many assume this will only occur after death,

The truth of the matter is that we cannot achieve it ourselves with any amount of control or discipline and certainly not with hard work. The right to come into the presence of Jesus is entirely a gift of God, not earned, not achieved, but simply accepted and adopted as a belief. Not only are we forgiven of our failings, we are offered the right to be one with him, to have his being within us and to partake in the unity of God. What he has promised he must provide, that is the very nature of God within us.

After the first time I experienced this vision, I have made this journey a part of my ongoing prayer life and have, to varying degrees, been able to enter again into the visionary temple of his presence. This was not directly linked to my death experience, but certainly has resulted from my attempts to rediscover the unity I felt with him at that time. In the past I would have attempted to achieve unity with God by concentrating hard, applying all my intellect and effort to control my mind and speak to him in the hope that he would hear and occasionally respond. There is nothing intrinsically wrong with this approach, in fact it is the natural human way to approach a God that is far greater than we are.

I have learned that by taking this approach we are in fact looking right past him and into the vast distance, when he is in reality so close we can touch him. The way becomes open when we are able to relax, stop 'trying hard' and allow ourselves to see with the mind's eye, truly be in the spirit and embark on the journey. If we simply surrender our will, our intellect, our hearing and our vision to him, then he will lead us to places where we could not dream it possible that we could go. It is important to realize that any spiritual vision will not come about through your own effort, but rather, it will occur when you are able to trust enough to allow him to lead you.

It has been my privilege to be led into the sanctuary of the spirit many times by seeking the kingdom of heaven within me, revisiting the places and feelings that I experienced while physically dead and drawing near to him in the simplest, most vulnerable and humble inner state by letting go control and allowing him to have the captaincy of my soul.

This requires time, quiet time on your own, dedication to the cause of finding him within and willingness to forgo intellectual control over your thoughts and visions. If you will not let go of the wheel, how can God steer the car? It involves surrender to the feelings within your heart and allowing them to flow freely. It involves faith to believe that God would make himself so readily available to you in your daily life, where you are sitting, right now. This requires the understanding that God is always with you, in every time, in every place, waiting to open the door and welcome you into the temple of his presence. If it seems too easy to be true, let me assure you it is not. It is easy. It is true. Heaven's gates stand open to you even as you read these words.

I can only encourage you to take the leap of faith and believe that God will guide the visions within you and provide you with an experience of his infinite love and his immanent presence. Why do we find it hard to believe that something infinite can be infinitely small as well as large, easily accessible and simple, natural and completely at home within us? We have been taught to believe in a God that lives beyond the sky in a distant kingdom called heaven and yet Jesus himself promised that he and his father would make their home within us. Is not their home heaven? Is not this a promise to bring heaven within us? Did not Jesus say, "the kingdom of heaven is within you"? We have access to him in a place that is so close to home that we continually overlook the obvious; that he is a part of us, and we are a part of him.

God inhabits the chambers of your heart and the corridors of your mind just as surely as he is in the wind and the clouds, just as surely as he sits on his throne in the heavens. Being infinite also includes you as a part of his limitless being.

Naturally we can access his infinite being from within us. Why would it be any less accessible from within us if it is truly infinite? We cannot go physically to the distant heavens, but with our heart and soul open there are no such limitations to those who are willing to be active in the spirit. To be one with Jesus is the greatest privilege a human being can experience. To ascend to the heavens upon and through the power of his spirit is a delight beyond words. I may not be able to ascend to the heavens in my body, but my spirit can be seated with him in the heavens.

"And God raised us up with Christ and seated us with him in the heavenly realms in Christ Jesus, in order that in the coming ages he might show the incomparable riches of his grace, expressed in his kindness to us in Christ Jesus." [Eph. 2:6-7 NIV]

The vision I have seen has established for me that there is a small rip in the veil between Heaven and earth. I have told you of this vision not to boast of any ability I may have as an individual, rather it is included with the aim of encouraging all readers to reach beyond the boundaries of their physical perception and to become familiar with the spiritual realm, the kingdom of heaven. Even now as I read back through my own experiences, I can see that to the everyday person this may seem far-fetched. My answer to that is yes, it is very far-fetched, very "out of this world." This is an account of what happened to me in the spiritual realm, written from the point of view of my spirit, of a person who was at those times operating in the spirit.

Keep in mind that much of the Bible was written as accounts of such spiritual encounters. Peter's vision of a sheet being lowered from heaven with all sorts of unclean animals led to the spread of Christianity throughout the Roman Empire and beyond. The entire book of Revelation was written by the Disciple John while in the spirit on the island of Patmos. A large proportion of the writings of the Old Testament prophets were descriptions of visions and words seen and heard while in the spirit.

Maybe it is a result of my death experience that I can now move more easily into the spiritual realm than I could before. I do not have an answer to that question. One thing I do know is that the power of this vision has inspired and excited me, awakening a drive and a desire to learn more about accessing the kingdom of heaven and to be closer to the presence of the Lord in any way possible. I thank God that he has given me a chance to experience even a small portion of his power through this vision and I will strive to re-enter his presence whenever he allows me to draw closer and see a brief glimpse through that tear in the veil and reaches into my heart to awaken that desire again.

It is my understanding that God greatly desires that we learn to function effectively in the spirit, that we see with spiritual eyes and hear with spiritual ears. As a child learns to understand and speak their native language, so we must learn to operate in the spirit, developing our abilities through much practice and experience. We should try again and again to activate and use the gifts God has placed within us, to aspire to the capacity we have been given to become truly spiritual beings through the grace of Jesus and the power of the Holy Spirit.

I hope this book inspires you to try and stir the spirit within you into flame and to burn brightly as you attempt to ascend beyond your physical existence into the kingdom of heaven. It is my wish and I believe also God's wish that you learn to transcend the cares and restraints of this life and see beyond the veil between the worlds into his magnificent domain. To live by the spirit is to overcome the limitations of a physical life. What after all are those limitations? An inability to see beyond earthly values into heaven's way of being, having faith only in the things we see, hear, smell feel or taste. If we choose to remain within the restrictive boundaries of physical life, disregarding all that is beyond our five senses, we are effectively locking the door to the kingdom of heaven.

God requires us to take a leap of faith to believe that we can see the invisible, to believe in the existence of another realm, spiritual rather than physical. Angels are the spirit messengers of God that inhabit heaven. On occasions in history they have made themselves visible to humanity and the veil between the spiritual and physical has been breached. Many prophets or seers have been taken into the heavenly realm to experience God's glory. It is not impossible that such things can take place in our lifetime. An eternal God does not alter his means of communicating with humanity simply because their attitudes have changed.

Heaven has not changed its character or its location, it is humanity that has shifted. To believe in the unseen, to see into the spiritual has been reduced by this world to the realm of illusion and delusion. According to the values of heaven those who have the eyes to see and ears to hear the heavenly kingdom are the chosen vessels of God's Spirit and those who bear the light of God into this world.

I am proud to have experienced the small moment of time I had in Jesus presence. I also feel blessed to have been able to experience the heavenly temple in a vision. I wish that every reader of this book could be blessed in the same way I have been. Yes, there have been dark and tragic days in my life but despite this the grace of God has given me a hope for eternal life in the spirit. Fear and sorrow fade away in the face of God's glory and are replaced by a joyful assurance that we are all loved, that through Jesus there is indeed a way to enter heaven and experience the infinite.

I believe that God is calling us now to break out of the shackles of the physical life and begin to see beyond into the heavenly realm. He is calling us to higher places where the limitations of our earthly thoughts can no longer hold us down. Belief is the key that opens that door. Faith is the motivation that carries us across the threshold. Trust is the assurance that we are welcome in his house. Jesus is the doorway through which we enter.

This is a call to action. If you read this book and simply place it on the shelf when you are finished, then I have failed. I seek to encourage you to change your understanding of what is possible and to inspire you to reach into the unknown recesses of your heart and soul, to explore the dark places of doubt and fear that may exist within you and shine the light of God into them. Yes, by all means close your eyes and submerge yourself in the visions of your soul while immersed in prayer. Hear the voices ringing deep within you and learn to discern the deep voice of God from among the mental chatter. See into the infinite possibilities that God paints onto the blank canvas of your soul. Let your heart open to the direct inflow of God's love and in turn let it flow out into the hearts of others.

This is not an intellectual exercise; this is a life-changing shift in your spiritual world. Don't only read of God and talk to God, see him, feel him, hear him and breathe him in. Let Heaven's breeze blow through the portal of your soul and refresh your entire being. Thank God for the awareness within you of his power and love and let that gratitude show in your life. Change, renew and reach upward and your whole inner being will be transformed. Clean out the dusty hallways of your soul and let God inhabit the space. Yes, it is simple and yes it is possible and yes it is invisible and powerful and uplifting. That is the nature of God's spirit and the effect he has on those who open the door to invite him in.

"Ask and it will be given to you; seek and you will find; knock and the door will be opened to you. For everyone who asks receives; he who seeks finds; and to him who knocks the door will be opened. [Matthew 7:7-8 NIV]

If we can but surrender our intellectual control and allow his spirit free reign within our inner being, we can experience his presence in a new and empowering way. I call on you to sit and dedicate time to enabling God to guide your mind's eye as he has with mine and reveal visions of the heavenly realm to you. Those that seek will find, to those who knock the door will be opened. May God bless you on your journey.

Printed in Great Britain
by Amazon

41128619R00081